8124

The Purpose of Politics

GW00546075

Oliver Letwin holds BA, MA and PhD degrees from the University of Cambridge; he was a Visiting Fellow in the Philosophy Department at Princeton University, and a Fellow of Darwin College, Cambridge. He has been a member of the Prime Minister's Policy Unit; he is currently Member of Parliament for West Dorset and an Opposition front-bench spokesman on constitutional affairs. He is the author of numerous publications including articles in learned and popular journals as well as *Ethics, Emotion and the Unity of the Self* (London, 1985), *Privatising the World* (London, 1986), *Aims of Schooling* (London, 1988), and *Drift to Union* (London, 1990).

The Purpose
of Politics

OLIVER LETWIN

The Social Market Foundation
May 1999

First published in English by The Social Market Foundation, 1999
in association with Profile Books Ltd

The Social Market Foundation
11 Tufton Street
London SW1P 3QB

Profile Books Ltd
58A Hatton Garden
London EC1N 8LX

Typeset in Bembo by MacGuru
macguru@pavilion.co.uk

Printed in Great Britain by Watkiss Studios Ltd

A CIP catalogue record for this book is available from the British Library.

Paper No. 40

ISBN 1 874097 34 8

Contents

III ARGUMENTS AND CONCLUSIONS

Preface

This little essay was once a long book. Serendipitously mislaid after ten years of intermittent work, a vast manuscript recreated itself as a slim volume without any noticeable loss of content – providing a ghastly testimonial to its author's prolixity. If, as a result of this history, the argument is now in places overly compressed, I hope the reader will at least bless the fact that the time required to negotiate the whole of it is short.

The origins of the essay lay in a perplexity – first felt as an undergraduate, subsequently amplified in the course of academic research and further intensified by professional involvement in politics. What, I asked myself, is politics *for*? And how does it relate to the things we *really* care about? Twenty years on, I have come to a conclusion – one that will be seen to owe much to Wittgenstein, Oakeshott and Berlin. This intellectual debt to the three towering figures of my formative years is perhaps unsurprising: it is the fate of ordinary mortals to know their own minds for the first time only when they have travelled far enough to return to the place from which they began.

It may be more of a surprise that, because I have restricted myself to answering my question single-mindedly, this is a book about politics which contains no reference to questions of economics, no discussion of political parties or of particular constitutional arrangements or types of regime, no discussion of rights and no detailed observations on the distribution of duties or rewards in society. I make no apology for these omissions: they are the topics of other works, not of mine.

I owe specific debts of gratitude to a number of friends, colleagues and audiences, on whom I have tried all or part of the ideas in this essay. I should mention, in particular, Lord Skidelsky and his colleagues at the SMF and Professor Ian Little who have brought about significant improvements of argument and style. My colleague, Robert Jackson MP, offered a trenchant critique which forced me to reflect further on several sections of the work. Two other scholars of distinction, Professor Daniel Bell and Dr John Marenbon, old friends and mentors, have laboured mightily to improve the draft and have succeeded in removing some of the most egregious defects. For those that remain, I am alone responsible.

I The Nature and Aims of
Political Action

1 False Gods

The aim of politics

What is the aim of politics? This question, in its sociological or historical form – 'what are the actual aims of those who engage in politics' – is, despite the valiant efforts of sociologists and historians, as nearly unanswerable as any question can be. There is no knowing who may enter politics or what, once they enter, they may be aiming at. But there is another, philosophical, form of the question – critically important for everyone who takes part in politics: 'what is the *proper* aim of politics?' This is an *ought* question, not an *is* question.

The question itself presupposes the answer to a prior question: 'has politics *got* an aim?' Is there, in other words, some one thing or one set of things at which all politicians at all times in all places ought to aim? Very many people think not. There are the cynics who think (even if they do not explicitly say) that politics is just the dirty business of self-enhancement cloaked in the disguise of high morality and that the only 'ought' in politics is that one ought not to take part in it. Thomas More, in one of his moods, half-believed this; there are probably tens of millions of ordinary men and women who would half agree with him. Then there are the 'pragmatists' – sometimes describing themselves as 'Tories' – who believe that the idea of a universal aim of politics is naïve and dangerous. 'Each time, each place, its own' is the banner under which they sail.

There is no general answer to the cynics and pragmatists. The only convincing way to refute them – if such a refutation is indeed possible – is to propose an aim for politics which transcends the interests of individual politicians, and to show why this aim ought universally to apply despite the acknowledged and fundamental differences between societies at different places and times. The purpose of this book is to identify such an aim and to show precisely such universality of application. Before embarking on the project, it is as well to recognise that many others have attempted the same task, implicitly or explicitly advancing particular, ostensibly universally applicable aims for politics. Alas, the wrecks of their endeavours are lying on the seabed of intellectual history; but they are instructive, helping to illustrate both the scale of the problem and – by omission – some of the lines of the solution.

Freedom

Ask a schoolboy what the aim of politics is, and if he has been brought up as a good liberal he will, like as not, tell you that the aim of all politics is to promote human freedom. This doctrine, taken straight, is empty. Liberty, unconstrained and unaccompanied by any of its best virtues, is valueless, vacuous and ugly. When a vandal, exercising his freedom, tears apart the Rubens in King's College Chapel, or when an existentialist murders his mother as an *acte gratuite* to show his capacity for authentic choice, or when a talented young person uses his liberty to destroy his talents by taking heroin, these are examples of freedom, but they are not desirable states of affairs. Any politics which aimed simply to promote freedom in this absolutely unfettered, and hence conceptually narrow, sense would be not only worthless but dangerous – a recipe for anarchy, mayhem and destruction. Whatever politics ought to aim at, it is surely something more and something better than that.

But the failure of freedom as a be-all and end-all of politics should not be allowed to obscure the vast significance of freedom as a *constituent* of the aim of politics. Wherever liberty has been too heavily constrained, the result has been catastrophe in both moral and prudential terms. In place of self-sustained standards, ethical and technical, come the sordid skills of currying favour with tyrants and the gloomy, downtrodden acquiescence of all but a few heroes. The fact is that men and women do not thrive in cages and the final proof of this truth comes at the moment of release. We who have witnessed in our own time the liberation of peoples from the yokes of tyrannies inevitably recognise the sense of relief so intense as to be describable only in music or poetry – the chorus of the prisoners in *Fidelio,* entering the light as they emerge from their dungeon.

These points do not need to be laboured: they are obvious, and implicitly acknowledged as such on every occasion when a political argument appeals to freedom as an end in itself. The *un*obvious point is the point of balance. If unfettered liberty is in itself valueless, vacuous and ugly, and if excessive constraint of liberty is a cause of moral and prudential catastrophe, where is the mean between too much and not enough? The question is not, of course, a new one. Indeed, a great part of the history of modern political theory can be understood as a series of attempts to answer it. Unfortunately, however, the two principal kinds of answer to date have been unsatisfactory. On the one side, there is what might be called the Aquinas/Locke/Hegel thesis; on the other, what might be called the Kant/Mill thesis. Proponents of the Aquinas/Locke/Hegel thesis argue that we human beings are, in one way or another, 'in touch' with a universal Reason. They claim that this contact enables us to 'intuit' the fundamental principles of Right, and that these intuitive principles set – at least at an abstract level – the proper limits to freedom, leaving only the problem of identifying in a given case the appropriate concrete, positive laws to embody the principles. The difficulty is that this 'only' problem – of identifying appropriate positive law – is crucifying. From the point of view of practical politics, vast, vague references to intuitions of universal Reason lead to no illumination and no agreement whatsoever on positive law. Whatever the dictates of Natural Law (if any) may be, they do not settle whether one person should be free to build a house that blocks the view of another, whether people should be allowed to sell drugs to one another, or what proportion of income people should be free to spend for themselves. Proponents of the Kant/Mill thesis attempt to solve this problem with a structural answer: that the limits of the freedom of one person should be set at the point at which that person's freedom interferes with the freedom of another. This thesis at least establishes a practical means of making political decisions. But, alas, the thesis (as has been frequently pointed out) is, if taken literally, a recipe not for modified freedom but for absolute tyranny, since *every* expression of one man's freedom is, in some respect, a constraint on the freedom of someone else – leading to the conclusion that no-one should be allowed to do anything. The paradox can, of course, be resolved by less literal interpretation of the Kant/Mill hypothesis, in which the principle is transformed into the proposition that one person's freedom should be limited at the point where it interferes *too much* with the freedom of others. But this transformed proposition leaves wide open the question of what constitutes 'too much' – and thereby returns, by a different route, to the vast terrain of unresolved questions bequeathed to us by the Aquinas/Locke/Hegel thesis.

The recitation in detail of the many deficiencies of the multitude of particular efforts to solve these difficulties by the application of ever-cleverer variants of the two basic hypotheses would be purely tedious. The essential problem is that the proper limits of freedom – the balancing point between freedom and constraint – cannot, from the point of view of practical politics, be derived systematically from some abstract principle. Life is, in this respect, more complicated than is dreamt of in even the subtlest philosophies. And yet, the truth behind these theories is that the proper aim of politics must include both the promotion of freedom (noting that too little is undesirable) and some limitation of freedom (noting that too much is undesirable). The aim of politics, once truly identified, must therefore be such as to explain how and where the proper limits of freedom are to be set.

Equality

Next to freedom, the item which is most frequently advanced, explicitly or implicitly, as the aim of politics is equality. The first point to be noted here is that – at least in the negative sense – there is something *to* the egalitarian thesis. All of us who have feelings and have grown up in modern, liberal, democracies, feel not only that there should be equality before the law and an equal right to compete on the basis of merit, but also that there is something wrong with a society that is too unequal in wealth or income, a society in which the rich eat caviar whilst the poor starve. The explanation for this deeply held sentiment may be *prima facie* obscure, and it is certainly incumbent upon any satisfactory theory of the ultimate aim of politics that it should provide such an explanation. But what is *not* in doubt is the sentiment itself: if we are true to ourselves, we must acknowledge that we think certain gross inequalities to be wrong. The question, therefore, is not whether a measure of equality, like a measure of freedom, is a vital ingredient in society, but rather whether equality as a positive goal can be said to constitute a proper, ultimate aim for politics.

In its crudest form, as a proposition put forward from time to time by practising politicians who have somewhat lost control of their eloquence, the assertion is that politics has, as its ultimate aim, the achievement of an absolute equality of outcome. Under the inspiration of this self-parodic ambition, the politician decries the least difference in circumstances between one person and another as a sign of a diseased society and stigmatises inequality of any variety without further argument. Every inequality is characterised as a gross inequity presumed to arise from the fact that some group or class of persons is exploiting the remainder of the population. Put under the glare of even a moderately powerful light, this assertion – which was probably hardly intended to be taken seriously by its rhetorical proponent – collapses entirely into incoherence. Absolute equality of outcome is clearly impossible without an almost unthinkably absolute and totalitarian tyranny which eliminates each vestige of difference as it occurs: a vision not only ghastly beyond measure but also inconceivable unless administered by tyrants, who would *ipso facto* be, in Orwell's memorable phrase, 'more equal than the rest'.

A rather less crude, and more frequently touted, aim is 'equality of opportunity'. As with absolute equality of outcome, this is an ambition more likely to be expressed by practising politicians than by political theorists – but by politicians of a calmer temperament or in a calmer mood. It sounds, at first hearing, so much safer and more reasonable an aim than equality of outcome. And yet, on inspection, its deficiencies both from a practical and from a theoretical standpoint become so manifest as to render it unworthy even of serious consideration.

Taken purely as an expression of the desire for equality before the law and for an equal right to compete on the basis of merit, 'equality of opportunity' is wholly unobjectionable, and – in modern, liberal societies – virtually uncontroversial. But, taken in this restricted sense, it can hardly be claimed to be the ultimate aim of politics: if only it were the ultimate end, we could all sit back and preen ourselves that politics had drawn to its conclusion long ago, with the good ship safely in harbour. The fact that politics continues – notwithstanding the widespread achievement of these goals – indicates that we do not see their achievement as in the slightest degree final.

The political proponents of equality of opportunity in fact sail under a much more ambitious banner: 'let each man and woman start life from the same position and make of it what they can': is their motto. Very well: so we must presumably abolish all inheritance (both genetic and proprietary); we must educate all children from the first moment of their lives, Plato-*Republic*-style in all-embracing school camps, removed from the dangerously unequal circumstances of what would otherwise be their unequal homes; and we must attend, as a matter of urgency, to the levelling of all differences which may threaten the perfect equality of the various school camps. All in all, a prospectus calculated to warm the hearts of tyrants and to chill the blood of their subjects. Nowhere in the world, as we have yet known it, has there been a tyranny so complete as this programme for strict equality of opportunity would require. Indeed, if faced with this *reductio,* the political proponent of 'equality of opportunity' will quickly retreat from the original assertion that such equality of opportunity is the absolute aim of politics, to a weaker and more plausible proposition – that some degree of equality of opportunity is one of the aims of politics, or that the presence of certain gross inequalities of opportunity is socially damaging: propositions which have real merits including the merit of truth, but which do not advance the cause of understanding what, if anything, is the true, ultimate aim of politics.

Ostensibly more satisfactory or, at any rate, more sophisticated attempts to answer this ultimate question are provided, as one might expect, by the major theorists of equality: the Marxists, the Benthamite utilitarians and the Rawlsian utilitarians. Put crudely, the Marxists identify the aim of politics as the elimination of the classes which differentiate men from one another and hence alienate them from their common humanity; the Benthamite utilitarians advocate, as the aim of politics, 'the greatest happiness of the greatest number'; and the Rawlsian utilitarians propose 'the benefit of the least advantaged'. Each of these formulations, as a form of egalitarianism, has something to recommend it. But, as a description of the ultimate aim of politics, each is seriously deficient.

Objections to the Marxist analysis of economic and political history can be raised at many levels: the Popperian attack – that the theory is not a theory because it at least attempts not to be falsifiable – has its power, as do the empirical efforts to provide what, in the case of any social theory, would count as particular falsifications, such as Trevor Roper's work on the English Civil War. There are also, regardless of the theoretic merit of these onslaughts against Marxist analysis, practical arguments against the Marxist claim that the proper aim of politics is an egalitarian struggle for liberation from class. As Lenin himself, and most subsequent proponents of practical Marxism, have recognised, a precondition for the supposed liberation is a (supposedly transitory) dictatorship of the proletariat.

Alas, the evidence of the past years has been that the super-abundance of wealth which Marx hoped to see is a chimera, and the dictatorship is neither transitory nor of the proletariat but rather a fully-fledged and, insofar as it is able, a self-perpetuating oligarchy imposing totalitarian tyranny. Nor can the ends, here, be separated from the means: 'liberation' from class and class consciousness involves, intrinsically, a total transformation of the way in which an entire people think of themselves and of their relation to family, friends and state – a transformation which cannot be wrought without totalitarian means. On these grounds alone, the aim must be suspect: nothing, one might reasonably argue, that requires *this* can be justified.

The direct theoretical attack on the Marxist egalitarian end is, however, deeper and more conclusive than any such indirect attack can be. The problem about the end is that it is not an end: it is merely an abandonment of the ship in uncharted waters. When Marx assures us that, following the liberation of man from the alienation of class-existence, the need for the state, and presumably for class as well, will cease, he is engaged in sheer fantastical millenarianism of the very sort for which he reserves his own most acerbic comments. There is no reason – outside of Marxist analysis – to suppose that social life between persons in a society will cease to require regulation. There is consequently no reason to suppose that life will ever avoid being subject to political decisions even if, as a result of an actually transitory revolutionary dictatorship of the proletariat, all members of society have been released from the shackles of class-consciousness. In other words, there would still be politics, and it would still have some proper aim. But Marxists do not even begin to tell us what that aim should be: they merely refer, for all their dismissive remarks about Utopian socialism, to a new Garden of Eden where unalienated men will work, rest and play in a state of unalloyed bliss. In the absence of the realisation of such a heavenly prospect, mundane politics remains – an enigma that cannot be explained by the Marxists.

Unlike the Marxists, Benthamite utilitarians give us a description of the aim of politics which is precisely designed to outlast all possible evolutions of society. And the aim in question – the greatest happiness of the greatest number – is undoubtedly egalitarian in the sense that it places no more weight on any one member of society than on any other: it recommends that each should count for one and that political decisions should be made on the basis of determining what course of action will, counting each for one, maximise the sum of happiness. The practical and conceptual difficulties with this theory are by now well explored. The most important difficulty is the absence of any known felicific calculus which might enable decision-makers to determine inter-personal utility – the extent to which the happiness caused for one person by a given circumstance outweighs or is outweighed by the unhappiness caused to another person by the same circumstance. It is not even clear that it is conceptually coherent to compare inter-personal felicity in this way: happiness, to the extent that it is an intrinsically subjective phenomenon, may be intrinsically unmeasurable since measurement requires objective comparison. Measuring happiness may be like asking whether your blue is bluer than my blue – a discussion whose longevity would be matched only by its vapidity.

But the problems of Benthamite utilitarianism as a description of the aim of politics do not end with the practical and conceptual difficulty of inter-personal comparison of utility. As has also been extensively illustrated in the course of recent philosophical debate about utilitarianism as an ethical theory, there is a deep problem about the handling of the concept of injustice. A strict 'act-utilitarian' interpretation of Bentham's principle could, if inter-personal utilities were measurable, lead to a conclusion that, in a given case, an innocent man should be hanged in order to promote the felicity of some much larger number of others by, for example, preventing a riot. It has been frequently – and, surely, correctly – pointed out that there is something *wrong* with a theory that so utterly ignores the force of the injustice committed against the innocent. Indeed, the flaw seems to be radical since strict act-based Benthamite utilitarianism fails to account even for the fact that we place *any* weight on injustice. The Benthamite question should be *purely* about whether the unhappiness caused for the one man is greater or lesser than the increase in happiness of the many: the fact that one man's unhappiness happens to have been caused by an injustice should be an irrelevance. This apparent lacuna in Benthamite utilitarianism as a description of the aim of politics – its inability to account for the concept of injustice – can, as the utilitarians frequently reply, be handled by the introduction of rule-utilitarianism which gives a value to claims of justice by asserting that the aim of politics should *not* be to promote, directly and in each event, the greatest happiness of the greatest number but rather to promote adherence to a set of *rules* (including the preservation of justice) which will generally, over time, lead to results desirable for the bulk of mankind.

Unfortunately, however, even this attempt to save Benthamite utilitarianism as a description of the ultimate aim of politics fails because it fails to account for the *absolute* value which we place upon the avoidance of injustice. The Benthamites simply cannot explain why, quite apart from any effect on the degree of universal felicity, a gross injustice is something which we believe it is *ipso facto* wrong for a political decision to cause.

Very recently, a more sophisticated form of utilitarian egalitarianism has been proposed – a form which addresses head-on the problem of justice, and which at the same time avoids the problem of felicific calculation. This is Rawls's implied assertion that the aim of politics is to minimise the dis-benefit of the least advantaged. Of all the variants of egalitarianism, this is surely the one that deserves the most serious consideration. There is something obviously *right* about the claim that an arrangement of society in which the least advantaged are best served is a just arrangement – and Rawls provides a powerful, almost conceptually unchallengeable, explanation for this seeming obviousness through his principle of the 'veil of ignorance': if, so the argument runs, one expects that a cardinal feature of the concept of justice is impartiality, then an arrangement of society which would have been approved by an impartial spectator has a strong claim to be just; and an impartial spectator standing behind a 'veil of ignorance', who had no idea where in a society he would find himself, would rationally favour any arrangement under which even the least advantaged were better off. As an identification of what it is we feel when we universally disapprove of too great an inequality in society, and hence as a description of our attachment to equality, this seems definitive: if a given social system benefits the least advantaged, how could one rationally want more equality than that?

Whom could any additional equalisation rationally be bene-fiting if it were disbenefiting the least advantaged?

The question, however, is whether even this highly sophisticated form of egalitarianism can successfully qualify as a description of the proper, ultimate aim of politics. There are several reasons why, for all its depth, it cannot. First and perhaps *least* conclusively, the thesis can be doubted on its own terms. One may ask, following Rawls, whether the impartial spectator behind a veil of ignorance would really – unless risk-averse – favour any arrangement so tilted towards the benefit of the least advantaged. If (this might be called the economist's objection to Rawls) the spectator were a rational optimiser, would he not 'risk-weight' each of his possible outcomes and choose, not a society in which the least well-off were better off but rather a society in which, on a risk-weighted and hence, presumably, a man-year-weighted-basis, he would be best off. In other words, Rawls's own claims that impartiality guarantees justice and that impartiality behind a veil of ignorance validates his principle of the benefit of the least advantaged can be turned against him and used as an argument that a just society is in fact one in which the pow-erful Benthamite principle of the greatest happiness of the greatest number applies – leading us back to all the notori-ous practical and conceptual problems surrounding the application of that Benthamite view. A more *fundamental* argument can, however, be marshalled against the claim that Rawlsian egalitarianism correctly identifies the proper aim of politics. The *fons et origo* of this argument is the observa-tion that justice itself, though doubtless a vastly important element in political life, is too narrow a description of the total aims of politics. This assertion – though directly a refutation of Rawlsian claims, and indeed, more generally, of utilitarian and egalitarian claims to have identified the ultimate aim of politics – is also, in itself, significant and deserves separate treatment, since theorists who are neither Rawlsian nor in any other respect utilitarian or egalitarian nevertheless advocate justice as the ultimate aim of politics. Indeed, justice is the point at which the great theorists of liberty (above all, Kant) and the great theorists of equality meet, and meet also with many a modern liberal theorist.

Justice

'Injustice is a form of wrong; and the removal of injustice is therefore the right aim of politics': so one might encapsulate a classical liberal argument. As with freedom and equality, we have to admit at once that there is something *to* this thesis. 'Injustice is a form of wrong' is an unchallengeable proposition. Moreover, an element of justice, in the sense of 'due process', is a necessary condition for social life. Someone who denies these things either does not understand the meaning of injustice or does not understand the meaning of wrong and/or the meaning of social life. And from this premiss, the consequence inevitably flows that 'the removal of injustice is therefore *a* right aim of politics'. A politician who can claim the removal of an injustice as his aim *has* a claim insofar as he is right; and, if there is nothing else to be said against the effects of his actions, his claim is beyond challenge. But the second hypothetical here is critical: the fact that the removal or prevention of injustice is *an* unchallengeable aim does *not* imply (as the liberal theorist may all too easily slip into letting it seem to imply) that justice is *the* right aim of politics.

There are, in fact, compelling reasons for denying that justice is an 'over-riding aim'. The first such reason is that justice is a purely formal criterion: being just is compatible in principle with being poor, ugly, stupid, ungenerous, unadventurous and unamusing, and a just society may nevertheless be one whose inhabitants live lives with all of these undesirable qualities. Even the Rawlsian principle of justice leaves open the possibility of a society in which, although the least advantaged are most benefited, this is at the expense of the vitality, beauty, wealth, excitement, and generosity of spirit of the society as a whole. It may be, of course, that such unfortunate concatenations do not generally occur, and that what benefits the least advantaged at the same time usually contributes to the life of the society as a whole: but such empirical observations, even if true, are irrelevant since, if Rawlsian justice, or justice in any other sense, were the ultimate aim of politics it would not matter whether the effects on other aspects of society were good, bad or indifferent. And, *per contra*, the fact that we *do* care about these other effects shows that justice is in fact not the be-all and end-all that the liberal theorists sometimes represent it as being. There is more to life than what is formally fair – not least, what is aesthetically fair – and politics cannot have as its sole aim an ambition so restricted as justice without threatening to restrict life itself to an intolerable extent.

The second reason why justice cannot be the ultimate aim of politics is Aristotelian and moral in character: namely, that the creation of a just society does not necessarily imply the establishment of virtue, and that virtue is as obviously *right* as is justice itself. Manifestly, in the same way that the removal of an injustice constitutes a *prima facie* argument for any political act, so the improvement of the virtue of the citizenry is, in itself, an unchallengeable reason for action. It is, quite simply, *better* that people should be good than that they should be bad, and hence a politics that makes us better is *ceteris paribus* a better politics than one that makes us worse. But a politics which seeks solely to promote justice will, or at least may, on occasion militate against the promotion of virtue. This is most obviously and most superficially shown by circumstances of the sort presented in the doctor's dilemma. Where two patients have a need for a scarce form of cure, and one is ahead of the other in the queue, but the second is a better man, a politics devoted to the formal requirements of justice will (or may) prefer the first claim, whereas a politics aiming to promote virtue will always prefer the second. More seriously, and more generally, a politics which aims at justice will penalise morally noble acts where these conflict with the formal requirements of justice (the conscientious objection of a Quaker, the disregard of rules under circumstances of exceptional need, or the rigging of a result to prevent an evil). By so doing, such a politics encourages in citizens the moral misapprehension that right lies simply in justice, that the quality of mercy is indeed constrained, that motive is significant only in relation to result and intentionality, and that the purpose of human society is purely to establish proper formal relationships between persons, with all morality confined to private judgement. It is a classical failing of classical liberalism that it welcomes these conclusions with open arms: the liberal concept of public justice, private virtue – whilst a better rallying-cry than public virtue, private vice – is nevertheless both impoverished and unrealistic. A society that places no public value on virtue will gradually tend towards being one in which the formalities of justice are unaccompanied by virtue, however hard particular private individuals may struggle to maintain a broader and more humane morality.

Justice is, in short, both too restricted and too external a thing to constitute the ultimate aim of politics. It does not allow either for the exuberant multiplicity of social values or for the call of the human heart and of human courage. It is a desiccated, empty husk that can be brought to life only by being filled with the liquor of virtue and surrounded by a cornucopia of other aspects of life.

Virtue

What, then, of the internal analogue? Can *virtue* qualify for the position left vacant by justice, and be truly represented as the ultimate aim of politics? This view of the primacy of virtue – the Platonic, Aristotelian, and Puritan conception of politics – has had a reasonable run, albeit almost entirely before the liberals put justice on a pedestal. But the problems with any claim for virtue as the ultimate aim of politics are even more acute than those associated with justice.

To begin with, there is the objection that such a politics attempts to make windows into men's souls. For the state to cultivate virtue, as opposed to the mere externality of just acts, the state must know the effects of its actions and influences upon the motives and attitudes of the citizen; it must therefore become an inquisitor – a Platonic tyrant, seeking to compel us to reveal all, and to order all aspects of our internal lives. In practice, this objection may not be very strong, since the state can, if it chooses, seek to improve the morals of its citizens not through direct intervention but through the indirect, and in principle less tyrannical, form of laws, leading men by habituation into the practice of virtue: such an approach is thoroughly compatible with the view of virtue as an ultimate aim of politics so long as one adopts also the Aristotelian thesis that virtue is acquired through the habit of practising virtuous acts. It is, indeed, this course which Aristotle and, perhaps, the Plato of the *Laws* rather than the Plato of the *Republic* recommend.

There is, however, a second, and more profoundly liberal objection to the concept of virtue as the ultimate aim of politics: the sceptical or relativist attack, based on the question 'who is to be the great law-giver that can be trusted to instil virtue in us all through the medium of the state?' No-one – so the sceptical argument runs – is in a position to offer such guidance to the rest of us because no-one has special access to a source of absolute truth sufficiently powerful and certain for such law-giving. Politics, the argument goes on, should therefore restrict itself to the externalities (justice, liberty, equality or whatever) on which men can in principle agree despite differing moralities. This argument is more powerful than the objection from tyrannical intervention because there is no doubt that the moralities of different groups of people within a given civil society do or may differ from one another. Any attempt to use politics and law as methods of reinforcing or reforming morals must therefore either ride roughshod over such differences or else restrict itself to those aspects of the multitude of moralities that are common to all, leaving the peculiarities of each to be reinforced by private or familial influence. But it remains highly questionable whether the objection is powerful *enough*. In any society which stands a chance of remaining intact for any length of time, there must surely be a considerable degree of common ground between the differing moralities within it; and if there is such common ground, then politics can be asked to articulate those common beliefs in laws and administrative acts which reinforce the common morality of the community.

The traditional liberal objections to the claim for virtue as the ultimate aim of politics are, then, too weak to be sustained in the face of hostile fire. But there is another objection − weaker in its claims and correspondingly stronger in its force − indeed, so strong as to administer an immediate knock-out blow. This is the assertion that whilst virtue may well be *an* aim of politics, it cannot be the *ultimate* aim because, though it is absolutely valuable, it is not the only valuable absolute that politics can deliver. The claims of other items − including at least prosperity, beauty, liberty, equality and justice − must also be heard. A society of overwhelmingly virtuous people in which the political arrangements nevertheless engender extreme poverty, grotesque ugliness, intolerable restriction, gross inequality and grave injustice would not be an ideal society by most standards. It would not be a society in which anyone other than a *nec plus ultra* Puritan would choose to live (and not, incidentally, a society in which Aristotle would have chosen to live). Proposing the inculcation of virtue as *one* of the most important things at which politics can aim is, therefore, altogether different and altogether more plausible than proposing virtue as the sole, ultimate aim of politics in comparison with which all other ambitions are to be dismissed as trivial. Collective Puritanism has its merits, but also its limits.

It might, of course, be argued by a die-hard proponent of virtue that a society which promoted virtue would also inevitably promote those other benefits for mankind; and this argument might involve either the assertion that virtue breeds all other goods or that virtue is bred only where other conditions of bliss are also present. But, regardless of the truth or otherwise of the empirical assertion on which either form of this argument is based, the argument itself is wholly vacuous since, if virtue were truly the ultimate goal of politics, it would be regarded as a sufficient achievement even if it were *un*accompanied by other goods. To put the same point another way: if virtue is valued as the ultimate aim of politics only because it brings in its train, or is itself brought in the train of, other goods, then the true description of the ultimate aim of politics must in some way identify and include those other goods and cannot consist simply of virtue.

Beauty and Truth

If virtue cannot, by itself, provide a sufficiently comprehensive goal for politics, can the more abstract perfections of beauty and truth fulfil the requirements? These two are best taken together, because they have a close affinity as concepts. They are linked not only by their positive evaluations (it being always, in itself, a good thing to be beautiful or true) but also by their being, as Keats reminds us, at certain points indistinguishable from one another (the beauty of a perfectly concise and conclusive argument or the powerful verisimilitude of a great novel).

The argument *for* the establishment of beauty and truth as the ultimate aim of politics is clear: a society with a politics which consisted in the full realisation of both beauty and truth would be cleansed of the impurities of ugliness and falsehood, would shine, glisten, gleam and glow, unsullied by the dingy and tawdry artefacts and practices with which human societies are in fact filled. What nobler or more complete aim, then, for politics than to promote universal beauty and truth, to the extinction of their opposites?

The first possible objection to this description of the ultimate aim of politics is that – in its abstraction – it fails to give weight to human vitality, indeed to life itself. It can, with at least some plausibility, be argued that beauty and truth are not cumulative. A world that contains more beautiful objects is not thereby more beautiful than one which contains fewer; rather, a world (a scene, a sculpture, a sonata) is beautiful if it is beautiful – if, that is, it contains nothing that mars its beauty. Similarly, a world, a book, or a library containing more true statements is not thereby the truer; rather, it is true if it contains nothing false. Hence, a politics which aimed, purely destructively (Savanarola-style) at the obliteration of everything ugly and false, might indeed achieve the aim of a world containing nothing but beauty and truth – and might achieve this heroic result by obliterating a great part, perhaps even the whole, of the human race and its artefacts. Who is to say whether a landscape returned wholly to a state of prehuman nature would be less ugly and less pregnant with falsehood than our present world? But this wholesale destruction, even if it could be shown to increase the purity of the beauty and truth of our world, is not something that most of us would welcome, still less accept as the ultimate aim of politics. We attach a weight to life, to vitality, to creativity, to energy which admits that ugliness and falsehood will sometimes result, and yet means that we would not wish to see these undesirable effects eliminated if the cause is the pure quiet of the inanimate.

A proponent of beauty and truth as the ultimate aim of politics might, however, counter this argument with the assertion that, although beauty and truth are themselves binary rather than cumulative, the creation of the beautiful and the establishment of the truth are themselves valuable: each additional thing of beauty, each additional truth revealed, having its own value. On this basis, vitality and creativity would be given back their place.

Indeed, a proponent of beauty and truth would be trying to create a politics in which, so far from the world being purified by the elimination of everything tinged by ugliness and falsehood, there was only the greatest possible encouragement for the creation of beauty and the discovery of truth. Savanarola would be replaced by Leonardo. The argument would be, not for the direct achievement – through direct purification – of a beautiful and truthful world, but for a politics which creates a framework within which the human genius for the creation of the beautiful and the discovery of truth is given the freest possible rein and every encouragement.

Even if the position is re-described in this way, though, the proponent of beauty and truth has significant difficulties in maintaining his claim for them as the ultimate aim of politics, because these ideals, in their abstraction, cut across the other values. Suppose, for example, that the pyramids are a work of great beauty, but that they could not be built except through the use, abuse and finally death of a vast number of slaves. Can it be the ultimate aim of politics to ignore entirely the demands of liberty and justice in order to promote the creation of beauty in this way? Similarly, if the truth of an important hypothesis in psychology or physiology can be tested only by experiments involving the involuntary vivisection of human beings, would it be part of the ultimate aim of politics to sanction or indeed encourage such experiments?

What these examples suggest is that, whilst the creation of beauty and the discovery of truth may be highly desirable, they cannot be said to be *ultimate* aims of politics since the pursuit of them has to be tempered or qualified by attention to other desiderata, such as justice and liberty.

Prosperity

At the opposite extreme from the claims of virtue, beauty and truth to be the ultimate aim of politics, we find the claim of prosperity: a material rather than an ideal condition.

To listen to modern politicians of almost all varieties talk in public, one would think that the search for the true aim could end here. Modern democratic rhetoric seems all too often to take almost for granted that prosperity is the aim of politics in a liberal state..... and yet somehow, somewhere we all have at the back of our minds, even in the midst of frenzied 'economic' debate, the clear certainty that this is a discussion of means not ends, that there is in some sense 'more to' politics than the mere pursuit of prosperity. Nor is it difficult to bring this certainty to the front of the mind, to articulate it in convincing particulars.

To start with, prosperity in the absence (or even the insufficient presence) of other desiderata itself becomes of dubious merit as a social aim, at worst a positive evil. We would not desire prosperity, nor ought we to desire it, if its precondition or consequence were the forsaking of liberty, the creation of inequalities that disadvantage the least advantaged, the perpetration of other forms of injustice, the encouragement of moral turpitude, the creation of ugliness, the inculcation of untruth – on and on goes the list of ends which, if compromised, make a mockery of prosperity. There is indeed 'more to' politics than prosperity, in the straightforward sense that prosperity is not enough.

Beyond this, though, prosperity, unlike the other desiderata, is principally of instrumental value. This is to say not simply that its desirability is compromised by conflict with other goals, but rather that it is valuable only insofar as it contributes to the achievement of those other goals. All of us, save the miser, aim at prosperity not for its own sake but because it opens the path to so much – to education, leisure, the widening of choice. Indeed, if prosperity has any non-instrumental value, this arises from its connection, at the extreme, with survival – an item which, in a money economy, is not strictly intensionally equivalent to prosperity but which is nevertheless so strongly the effect and measure of prosperity as almost to constitute its essence. But it would be a brave man who attempted to argue that, at least for societies in which survival is well assured, the point of all the attention to politics is or ought to be mainly the pursuit of survival. To make such an argument would, after all, be to argue effectively for the reduction of human life to the condition of being a tree or a mouse. There is 'more to' politics than prosperity in the further sense that a great part, at least, of the point of prosperity itself is to go beyond itself – beyond mere survival – towards other goals. As a description of the ultimate aim of politics, prosperity is woefully lacking.

And yet, once the insufficiency of prosperity as an ultimate goal has been acknowledged, the reality of its central importance has also to be recognised. By itself, nothing, empty, vapid; but without it, at best an unpleasing holiness and at worst disease, ceaseless work, hunger, irrepressible loneliness, the war of each against all. Somehow, and in a sense that must, to judge by its not having been articulated, be difficult to articulate, the importance of prosperity is at the centre of the riddle. It is not, cannot remotely plausibly be presented even as a candidate for being, the ultimate aim of politics; but it *matters,* and any proper account of the ultimate aim of politics must recognise and explain that mattering.

Power

Whereas prosperity, as a material ambition, stands at the opposite end of the spectrum from the moral aims and from beauty and truth, 'power' lies outside the spectrum altogether. The assertion that the ultimate aim of politics is power has not found much favour with serious political theorists. Both Hobbes and Machiavelli have been accused of advancing the retention of power by the ruler as the aim – in the sense of the *proper* aim – of politics. But anything more than a superficial reading suffices to show that neither Hobbes nor Machiavelli intended any such suggestion. In Hobbes' case, the purpose (the *proper* aim) of politics is undoubtedly seen as the establishment of a peaceful order within which human society can flourish. It is perfectly clear that, for Hobbes, power is to be established only for the sake of peace and to be transformed through recognised procedure into authority so as to become the basis for justice. And in Machiavelli, the advice to the Prince is to be seen not as a description of the ultimate proper goal of politics but rather as a series of prescriptions for the means by which a ruler is able to establish and retain a sufficient grip upon the state to enable him to govern – again, as with Hobbes, power is seen as a precondition, not as the ultimate aim.

Nevertheless, in the popular press and in a certain kind of loose conversation, the opinion is frequently expressed that 'all politics is about the effort by politicians to retain power'. Taken as a sad commentary on the deficiencies of modern politicians, this may be either true or cynical. But sometimes, it may express a deeper and more interesting, if more worrying, thesis or assumption: that there *is* no proper, ultimate aim of politics – that politics can only be (and hence, presumably, ought only to be) the pursuit of power because any attempt by politicians to identify or pursue another aim is doomed to fail. This thesis has a sufficient hold on popular discussion to be worthy of at least a cursory refutation.

The thesis would presumably, in its 'best' form be that each of the possible goals so far enumerated – liberty, equality, justice, virtue, beauty, truth, prosperity – is in its perfection unattainable. There will be at least elements or patches, if not vast tracts, of constraint, inequality, injustice, vice, ugliness, falsehood and poverty in a society. To remove these is, so the argument runs, beyond the capacity of man. Therefore, politicians had best stick to the one thing they *can* do: retaining power. Reduced to its essentials, this argument becomes the combination of two propositions: (1) perfection is unattainable and therefore (2) don't bother to make things better. Put in this form, one does not need to be an advanced student of logic to see the *non sequitur*. The attempt to aim at socially desirable goals is not proved to be futile by the fact that these goals are very unlikely to be achieved in their entirety – any more than the futility of building a fast train would follow from the fact that the speed achieved will not be infinite. Progress towards a goal is rational even if the goal itself is beyond reach.

However, the fact that power-seeking is not validated as an ultimate aim by the unattainability of perfection in relation to other aims leaves intact the significance of Hobbes and Machiavelli. For, Hobbes and Machiavelli, in forsaking liberty, equality, justice, virtue, beauty, truth and prosperity as individual goals – in refusing to speculate about a particular, ultimate goal of politics – gesture towards the conclusion (shared by other sceptics including, in our own time, Oakeshott), that the proper, ultimate aim of politics is no one of these qualities of life, nor any other such single quality but rather a manifold.

This conclusion – that politics is to be conceived ultimately as a pursuit leading to the establishment of an authority that will support not a single aim but a manifold of aims – is indeed a profound perception that leads directly to the very question which it is the purpose of this book to answer. If the claims individually of liberty, equality, justice, virtue, beauty, truth and prosperity to be *the* ultimate aim of politics cannot be sustained, and if the fostering of each of these qualities nevertheless has *a* claim to be *an* aim of politics, and if the obvious conclusion is that a manifold rather than a single quality must be the ultimate political desideratum, then what is the *nature* of the manifold, and how does the conduct of politics relate to its achievement?

The first part of the answer proposed by this book is that the manifold in question is the mysterious item which we call civilisation. But before that answer can be made plausible, a description of the nature of civilisation is required.

2 The Nature of Civilisation

The essential features of civilisation

What are the hallmarks of a civilised life? It is a horribly difficult question.

The first approximation to an answer can be derived from considering the opposite of civilisation – barbarism. We are told that the ancient Greeks identified barbarians by the simple expedient of listening to their discourse: if not in a recognisable tongue, it was held to consist of inarticulate grunts 'bar ... bar'. Whether this tale is history or merely a tale, it is conceptually accurate. The first mark of the barbarian – of any form of life which is not civilised – is the absence of articulate language. Whatever civilisation is, it necessarily includes the presence of language, the means of communication, the means of formulating, expressing and recording thought.

From this single beginning – articulate language – many of the central features of civilisation can be deduced either as preconditions or as consequences. A primeval Adam, devoid of his Eve, sprung unimaginably from nowhere, could not be supposed to have had a use for or the use of language. Meaning, as Wittgenstein never tired of pointing out, derives from social practice: it is because I use words in ways that others recognise, that I can communicate, have recognisably a language. A lone being – not stranded like Robinson Crusoe, but created alone *ex nihilo* – would neither need, nor be able to create, language, because his words would be without the external context of social practice and social recognition needed to give them meaning. So it follows, from the necessity of language to civilisation, that civilised existence must be by origin and essence a social existence – an existence in which one person is related to another. This is not, of course, to deny the hermit a role in civilised life, but rather to recognise that what makes the hermit civilised is his emergence from a nexus of social relations and his carrying with him into his hermitage a myriad of inheritances from those social relationships. In other words, civilised man may not live in society, but he is at root a social animal that has grown up in society.

The fact that civilisation depends on language and hence on society has other implications. A society cannot exist without at least a modicum of peace and stability. In a perpetual Hobbesian war of each against all – if such a state of affairs can be imagined – people would not be able to do more than struggle for individual survival. A language is possible only because, within groups of at least some size (whether constituted by family, friendship, clan, city or state) we establish a co-existence sufficiently peaceful to permit the evolution of relatively stable expectations and recognitions. We can talk to one another because we have created time and space in which to learn to talk, and because we have created a degree of peace within which our talk can result in reasonably predictable responses on one another's part. This in turn implies, as a necessary precondition for civilisation, a degree of social organisation sufficient at least to preserve the peace within the group whose language is held in common, and sufficient to preserve that group for at least a period against attack from without. From the necessity of language, then, we can draw out as necessary features of civilisation: society, a degree of stability, and a degree of social organisation.

These items, language, society, stability, social organisation, should not, however, be conceived as static. They subsist not merely at a moment but over time: a civilisation depending on language, depends on history, both on the history of the evolving society which make possible and forms the language and on the history of the language itself. This is inevitably a *shared* history. It is only to the extent that the speakers of the language share their linguistic history that they can communicate. And it is only because, and to the extent that, they share in a common social history that they can have the stability of expectation and recognition which is the foundation of articulate communication in language.

A shared linguistic and social history is more than an external inheritance. It is a form of life – a state of common, mutually expected and mutually recognised practices promoting a state of common understanding. In a civilised society, people use signs and symbols with narrow rules of expectation and recognition: using the sign or sound 'yes' to signal the affirmative, and so on through countless numbers of common practices. Some of these practices will be directly linguistic, others will form part of the fabric of the social organisation which promotes the peace and stability that alone makes possible the continuity of a history within which language can be preserved and can evolve. Because human beings cannot centre their lives around a set of conscious acts without being themselves affected by the complex of their own activities, these shared practices are inevitably internalised to the point where they become at least partly constitutive of the individuals who engage in them. My use of language is not merely an external feature of my being; it is part of what I am as a subject. My thoughts, though my own, are thought in, and hence, to some degree, created out of our common language. In using the same language as you, therefore, I am sharing a form of life with you – for each of us, part of what we are is that which we share between us. A civilised existence is thus not merely one in which individuals are socially related to one another, but also one in which individuals are (at least in part) formed by that social relationship. The civilisation lies not merely in the external relationship between us, but in the fact that as a part of having these relationships, we are as a matter of self-definition inheritors of the shared inheritance, speakers of the common language.

What is true of practices is true of principles. Indeed, at this level of abstraction, principles and practices meld into one another. It is impossible to say whether, within our society, the training of children not to murder, and the continuation of that training through the general acceptance and enforcement of law constitute a set of practices (all of these features of our lives certainly being practices) or a set of principles (the abhorrence of murder certainly being a principle). The truth is that the principle is expressed in, lives through, the practices, whilst the practices are informed by and are expressions of the principle. The principle *is* the practice in a sense that it is the abstract corollary of the concrete acts which, in their variegated repetition, constitute the practice. In recognising the practice *as* a practice, one *ipso facto* recognises the principle as that which informs and is expressed in the practice. Thus, in a society which shares moral practices, there is, to the degree that the practices are genuinely shared rather than merely coincidentally overlapping, a sharing of moral principle. Without at least a high degree of such shared principle, the peaceful coexistence and the stable framework of expectation which make possible a shared language would be unthinkable. The shared morality of our society − the sharing, that is, of certain ideas of what, in the crudest possible sense, is absolutely right and wrong − is therefore an indispensable precondition of the existence of our society as a civilised form of life.

The inter-relationship of civilisation and shared value is, however, deeper than this picture of the necessity of sharing values implies. Civilisation is not merely necessarily dependent on shared value: it is also, as a result, a source of value. To be civilised is to be part of, and to be in some degree defined as an individual by participation in the shared practices, which are constitutive of a society. An individual who is part of a civilised society is thus in part defined as an individual by adherence to the principles which, through his practices, acceptances and recognitions, he expresses in his life. To be a civilised person, in other words, is to be imbued with the values of a civilisation. Any one of the values with which I am imbued and which are in part constitutive of me, I may examine and even with difficulty and nostalgia amend or alter – altering, as I do so, my own practice. But to deny these values wholesale is to launch myself on a sea of indeterminacy in which my individuality, the coherence of my personality, can only be lost. I, as a civilised being, cannot continue to be myself if I constantly abandon *all* of the characteristics which I have inherited as part of becoming what I am. My relationship, at any given moment, to my society, is therefore in part at least a relationship of source and application. In my practices, expectations and recognitions, I am applying the values of which my society through its shared inheritance is the source. A civilised life is, in short, one in which absolute value is granted in common principles.

In pure theory, common principles could take any form: a society might exist on the basis of principles and practices which, for example, place no value whatsoever on any object external to the individual subject as an end in itself. Such a society could be one in which the individual would simply and continuously seek to exploit the totality of his surroundings (including, here, other members of the society as part of the surroundings) to the optimal point – the point at which his own desires were satisfied. Whether, in practice, a society formed of such principles would be feasible is an interesting question, which, however, need not detain us. The significant point is that such a thorough-going instrumentalism would at best present the *appearance* of being civilised. Civilisation in any full sense requires each individual to recognise external features of the world as ends in themselves. When Kant defends the centrality of the concept of an end in itself, he is defending one of the central pillars of civilisation. We call vandalism against works of art, the burning of books, the fail-

ure to recognise and appreciate emotion, marks not of civilisation but of barbaric life. When we speak of 'civilised conduct', we call to mind a form of life in which other beings
are recognised as having 'equivalent centres of self', in which,
indeed, the shades of emotion of those other beings are reg-
istered with some sensitivity, in which art and knowledge are
valued for their own sake – in which, in short, the whole
world is *not* reduced to an instrument for getting and spend-
ing but in which on the contrary there is a full recognition
of the value of the non-instrumental (of feelings felt without
ulterior purpose, of beauty seen as beautiful and not as
useful, of all other human lives considered as ends in themselves). To be civilised is to share not merely a value-system
but also a value-system which does not treat everything as a
means to some other end.

The relationship of one civilised perception to another is
worth understanding, since, once clarified, it helps to delin-
eate the boundaries of civilisation and barbarism. On the one
side, it is commonly supposed (and not without some reason)
that an individual who is civilised in the sense of recognising
the value of one of the more abstract non-instrumentalities
(for example, the beauty of a great work of art, or of a sunset)
will be likely also to be sensitive to the non-instrumental
value of other persons and of the shades of their feelings. On
the other side, it has to be recognised that abrupt discontinu-
ities can occur. The commandant of a concentration camp
might have been a lover of Beethoven's music; a person of no
aesthetic sensibilities may nevertheless have a fine sensitivity
to the significance of other persons and to their feelings.
Neither of these common observations is surprising.

Together, they amount to saying that, whilst one aspect of civilised life may frequently encourage others, elements of barbarism can quite sustainably persist in a single individual or indeed in a society as a whole. One cannot, therefore, talk of a person or of a society as simply 'barbaric' or 'civilised' – one must rather identify the aspects which are civilised and those which are barbaric. The progress from barbarism to civilisation is, in other words, a continuum: any society with sufficient stability to have evolved, through a shared history, forms of social organisation and common practice to the point where language is sustained, has some claim to be other than purely barbaric. As the embodiment in practice of evaluative principles becomes stronger, as the forms of social organisation become richer, as more and more recognition is given to the value of persons, feelings, and beauty as ends in themselves, the claim of the society to the status 'civilised' becomes increasingly strong.

On the road from unimaginably pure barbarity to unattainably pure civilisation lies another aspect of our lives – our openness to truth. In a fully civilised society, practice is not simply act; it is also brought into conscious belief by self-understanding – reflection of historical, sociological, philosophical and critical varieties. Through these abstract enquiries, and through some of the forms of art, we picture – in a high civilisation – ourselves, our past and our future to ourselves. The external world, too, is pictured through the many branches of science. And these forms of knowledge – this is a hallmark of high civilisation – are not merely used as part of the effort to seek comfort, health or warmth, but are also valued in themselves as items endowed with non-instrumental value, analogous to the value of individual life and feeling or of natural and artificial beauty. The barbarian knows nothing, and cares nothing. The civilised person in a civilised society is surrounded by, and imbued with, both knowledge and the love of knowledge. We recognise the Athenian promotion of thought as a characteristically civilised phenomenon and the stamping out of thinking by the hordes of Genghis Khan as a characteristically barbaric activity.

The close relation of civilised life to the value of individuality, beauty and truth as ends in themselves leads to a most interesting paradox which has been far too little explored in the history of social thought: the paradox that a civilised society is one in which so much attention has been paid to the generation of wealth, and so successfully, that attention can be, in great part, diverted from that pursuit to the creation and appreciation of beauty, and the pursuit of knowledge. Where (as in ancient Greece) the creation of wealth lags behind aesthetic and intellectual achievement, a highly civilised existence, if it occurs at all, will be available only to a restricted group whose leisure is derived by treating the rest of society as a means to an end.

These, then, are the essential features of a civilised society: an inheritance of shared practice and shared value, the treatment of persons as ends rather than means, and the use of prosperity to pursue beauty and truth. Since both the complete absence and the complete fulfilment of these attributes are in practice equally implausible, history in fact consists of societies that are to differing degrees civilised. The progress from barbarism to civilisation is a continuum.

This civilisation

It is one thing for a society to be civilised, quite another for it to be *a* civilisation. Being a civilisation implies being, recognisably, *this* civilisation rather than some other. The question thus arises: is there such a thing as *this* civilisation as opposed to some other? Is civilisation a phenomenon that comes in discrete packets, or is being civilised more like being yellow − a quality that attaches? There can, surely, be no doubt of the answer: a civilisation is a discrete phenomenon. We speak regularly of modern European civilisation, Ancient Chinese civilisation and so forth − denoting a time and place at which a particular civilisation can be said to have existed. When speaking in this way, we reveal our belief that whilst 'being civilised' is a universally recognisable and highly general quality involving shared inheritances of the forms already identified, there are nevertheless particular civilisations, demarcated by their differing inheritances, differing languages, customs, values, forms of life. This is indeed commonplace. What is not so obvious is how the differing civilisations are related to one another. Where does one civilisation begin and another end? If civilised life consists of shared inheritances, how shared must they be to constitute a discernible unit of civilisation? How disparate must they be to constitute discernibly different civilisations?

The image required here is that of a kaleidoscope. Observe the kaleidoscope at a given moment: it contains a multitude of patterns and patterns of patterns − each different, composed of different elements and together constituting, at that moment, a single grand pattern. Shake the kaleidoscope gently and one or more of the patterns slightly alters. Shake it again, more vigorously, and patterns begin to open up and dissolve into one another. Eventually, they re-form, until at last the pattern as a whole is radically altered and only the observer, with his knowledge of the sequence, can testify to the connection of the present with its past. So it is with civilisation. Each element, and each sub-pattern of which that element is a part, has its meaning, its place in the universal picture, as a result of its participation in larger pat-terns – and each element comes to have that meaning through the evolution over time of its relationships with the other elements in the patterns of which it is a part. It would involve a fruitless effort to disintegrate what is in fact inte-grated to say that the civilisation of a certain English village in 1997 is separate from the civilisation of a particular village in France in 1893. To a degree, they are merely part of wider patterns of shared inheritance – European civilisation. But they are also separate – not only through their participation, respectively, in English and French civilisations but also through the inheritances which each village itself, at a time, can call its own. Both their connections and their separations are historically determined: the inheritances that they share, as much as the inheritances that differentiate them, have come into existence through the continual adjustments of the kaleidoscope.

The kaleidoscopic development of civilisations ensures their inter-penetration at innumerable levels. Thus, for exam-ple, post-colonial India is at once a product of ancient indigenous and more remotely imported civilisations and an extended part of modern European civilisation. To see modern Indian civilisation, one must understand how these originally very separate patterns were rudely shaken into one another, first by conquest and then by the development of communication, transport and an international intelligentsia. As a result, it makes no sense to speak of the civilisation of 'this place' – one must rather speak of the civilisation of this place *at this time,* and one must recognise in its historicity the extent to which it is in fact the embodiment of inheritances partly shared with other civilisations that have been in one way or another, to some degree or other and at some time or other, linked with it by the turns of the kaleidoscope.

The derivation of the meaning of the particular from the general is as essential a feature of the kaleidoscopic relationship between one civilisation and another as is their mutual and often inter-linked historicity. To a degree, all civilisations – simply by virtue of *being* civilised and of sharing, in consequence, at least some of the necessary features of civilised life – are part of the grand pattern. And this most generally and absolutely shared inheritance is at the same time the most fundamental of the inheritances of each civilisation. A particular civilisation is what it is in the first place because it *is* a civilisation – a collection of shared inheritances capable of acting as a source of value, and involving to some extent at least a recognition of the value of non-instrumentality. Only slightly less fundamental, a particular civilisation is what it is by virtue of embodying very general and most widespread historically shared inheritances – religion, moral principle, cognate or literally shared languages. It is only at a relatively superficial level that a civilisation is differentiated from others within the grand patterns of which it forms a part; and at the point where the society is dissolved to the individual, the idea of civilisation altogether evaporates. Thus, our society may be absolutely at root a civilised society, endowed with language and value, but may be only slightly less fundamentally an example of modern Western European Judaeo-Christian civilisation; more superficially, it may be born of the particular historicity of England; almost trivially, by comparison, it may be a civilisation of Birmingham or Wootton-Under-Edge (already an almost laughable idea); and it cannot be said with any meaning that Mr X, one particular inhabitant of Wootton-Under-Edge, is constitutive of his own single-person civilisation. This is not, of course, to deny in the slightest that Mr X is an individual, capable of making his own choices in his own life; it is to say rather that the context within which he does so is the civilisation of which he is – spiritually and mentally – an embodiment; in the depths of his mind, he is a civilised being, deriving moral sense from his Judaeo-Christian inheritances, speaking English, having grown up amidst the customs and forms of life of Wootton-Under-Edge. And just as his being civilised, his having moral sense, are more fundamental to an appreciation of *what* he is than his speaking English, so his speaking English is more fundamental to an appreciation of what he is than his having grown up in Wootton-Under-Edge.

Because the most general aspects of a civilisation are the most fundamental, they are the most inescapable. As an individual living within a civilisation, I am in part constituted by that membership: I am in part almost literally a 'member', in the sense of an organ or partial embodiment of that civilisation. I may, of course, change my language of use, my habits, my ways of life: but I cannot do so without a conscious effort of rejection, and in rejecting, I affirm, as part of the personal history which constitutes myself, the present possession of the very items that I am in future to abandon. I may, perhaps, learn to think, to speak, to feel in different ways, but I cannot do so, without at first (indeed over a protracted period), understanding these new ways precisely as 'different', as 'other' than my own. And, even with such conscious effort, it is to be doubted whether I can successfully jettison those aspects of civilisation which constitute the framework of my mind and spirit – the sense of moral value, the conception of non-instrumentality, the tenets of logic. Can I, as an embodiment of the civilisation of modern Western Europe, successfully persuade myself that it is right to copy the Samurai in testing a new sword by cutting off the head of the first villager with whom I come into contact, or successfully convince myself of the Buddhist proposition that the aim of life is oblivion? If such alterations of world-view are possible at all, then they are possible only with heroic energy – and for reasons which, in themselves, are bound in the first instance to have come from within the civilisation from which I start.

The shallowness of the particular, and the depth of the general, within a civilisation can be understood, in short, as a consequence of the increased inescapability of the general. It does not cost me much to escape from that which is shared as an inheritance only with the inhabitants of my little village: a local custom, a mode of speech. But to escape from that which is the shared inheritance of the great civilisation of which the life of my little village is a slight embodiment – from, for example, the fundamental moral sense of the Judaeo-Christian world, or from the conception of beauty as

45

an end in itself, is, if not impossible, very nearly so. This observation in turn leads to the recognition that there are, within any given civilisation, principles so deep as to be almost inevitably affective for those who are part of it. And it is this recognition which forms the beginning of a true understanding of the nature and role of the tensions within a civilisation.

The tensions within a civilisation

The essential and irremediable problem of a civilisation arises from the fact that those attitudes which are most fundamental to it are at the same time the most general and abstract. As a result, coherence is – by necessity – continually under threat in a civilisation. The value of beauty, for example, cannot within our civilisation be escaped; nor can the value of the individual as an end in himself. But no guarantee can be given that the first of these values will cohere with the second. Indeed, in many cases, the first will pull in one direction, and the second in another. The desire of the individual to tear down an 18th century house in order to build himself a swimming pool runs directly into conflict with the desire of 'the community' to see works of beauty retained intact. There is, here, in the conflict of two general principles, both deeply embodied in our civilisation, no 'right answer'. We place a value both on beauty and on individual preference. In this case, and in many others where prosperity, beauty, truth, liberty, equality, virtue, justice, the fundamental generalities of our civilisation conflict in the particular, no absolute guarantee of resolution is possible. Rather, there is a tension: something to be said on *both* sides, and no obvious means of deciding between them. Each of the claims affects us in opposing directions: we are strung, under tension, between them. As members of the civilisation, we cannot escape from the tension, because we cannot escape from the principles – as members of the civilisation we find the tension is *within* us rather than external to us.

These inescapable tensions are a problem for a civilisation, rather than merely a feature of a civilisation because, whilst the tensions can and do persist *sine die* without being capable of resolution at the abstract level, they have to be resolved by some means where they conflict in practice, if the civilisation is to remain intact. The failure to resolve them in practice, can lead only to warfare. The failure to recognise their force – the effort by members of a civilisation to 'pretend away' some of the claims – can lead only to barbarism. If you and I cannot find a way of resolving the clash between my desire to ensure that a virtuous example is set by what is published and your desire to promote dissemination of the truth, we can only fight it out. If either of us makes an effort to avoid the clash by pretending that either virtue or truth is of no account, a fundamental tenet of our civilisation is under attack, and barbarism is not far off. These claims must thus be recognised, seen to be in tension with one another in particular cases and somehow resolved amicably, or at least peacefully, in each particular case if our civilisation is to survive.

The distinction between such a fundamental tension and a clash of interests is both critical and difficult to discern. Mr A wants to build a supermarket in a field; Mr B, whose field it is, objects. Is this an instance in practice of the ever-present tension in a civilisation between prosperity and beauty? Or is it simply a clash of what is convenient to Mr A and what is convenient to Mr B? It may be no easy matter to decide: it may be that motives as well as rhetoric are mixed, in part appealing to the fundamental tension, in part to the clash of self-interest. Nor can it be guaranteed that the manifestations of the tensions, when they do occur, will take the form of 'clean' disputes between one principle and another. All too probably, several different claims will be involved in a polygonal tension − a cat's cradle of opposites, inter-mingled in part with, and perhaps difficult to disentangle from polygonal clashes of personal self-interest. There is no escaping, within our civilisation or any other, the eruption of such 'messy' disputes. Our shared inheritance is value-laden, and the values are no more consistent in practice than our interests.

The tensions between the fundamental principles of our civilisation are not, however, to be understood *solely* as problems. They are also dynamic and creative forces. It is by the finding of resolutions between them, as Burke says, that the laws and institutions of a society are given shape. At points where the tensions erupt into open clashes, means of bringing these clashes to a peaceable conclusion are found, and these means − typically laws or institutional arrangements − establish new balances of power between the opposing forces. The claim of prosperity is favoured at the expense of the claim of beauty, or vice versa in particular kinds of circumstances, by laws or institutions which give more weight to the one or the other when judgements or decisions relating to such circumstances are being made. As, over the course of history, clashes occur in a wide range of concrete instances, a set of laws and institutions is gradually developed.

These laws and institutions give order to the cat's cradle of tensions, establishing relatively fixed relationships between its various strands – thereby not only setting limits (albeit temporary limits) to future clashes, but also forming to a great degree the character of the society in which the civilisation is instantiated.

It is important to recognise that the skein of practical resolutions of the tensions in specific circumstances is not in any sense a 'second best': messy as it may be from a theoretician's point of view, it is absolutely the best that any human society can achieve, precisely because the tension between the principles cannot be resolved at an abstract level. At that level, the tension is and remains irresolvable: beauty and prosperity, liberty and equality are intensionally distinct and will all too frequently prove to be extensionally at odds with one another. But their status is equivalent; there is not, and there cannot be within a civilisation a compelling abstract argument favouring any one of the principles over the others. The resolution of the tensions in practice, through social institutions that have arisen out of particular clashes, is therefore the *only* means of recognising and at the same time constraining within any civilised limits the tensions that are an intrinsic feature of civilisation. Practice, here, Hegel-style, rescues abstraction. It makes possible results which are at the abstract level impossible.

The forms of change within a civilisation
It would be altogether a mistake to think of the tensions created by the various principles as merely an evil, to be fended off through constant vigilance. True, the tensions cause anxi-

ety and require containment if, what Berlin calls, the precarious balance of civilisation is to be maintained. But the tensions are also the agents of change, the great dynamic force within a civilisation. The way in which a civilisation resolves the tensions at a concrete practical level, and the extent to which at any given time a civilisation fully recognises the conflicting claims of the principles within itself, ultimately determines that civilisation's strength and vitality.

At its best, change within a civilisation consists of the peaceful implementation of new resolutions, within the framework of prior resolutions, following the successful capture of the imagination of society by the advocates of a particular principle. Recent examples, in our lucky societies, abound: the triumphant assertion of the egalitarian requirement for a social safety net against the principle of liberty; the belated acknowledgement of the principle of natural beauty against the claims of equality, liberty and prosperity. These massive shifts in popular consciousness and in the social definition of the acceptable have been, by and large, peacefully achieved within the framework of prior resolutions. The constitutional and legal procedures under which they have been resolved have mainly been recognised and obeyed both by the advocates of the newly emphasised principle and by the supporters of the principles whose practical effect has been diminished.

A civilisation is not always so lucky. From time to time, the tension between opposites may become unbearable and the framework of prior resolutions may not be sufficiently strong to guide the participants towards peaceful compromise. This is particularly likely to be the case when the logic of a principle that has captured the imagination of a society creates doubt about the legitimacy of the framework of prior resolution. Thus, for example, the Tolpuddle Martyrs no doubt felt that the failure of society to acknowledge the justice of their cause itself established the injustice of the existing framework for the peaceful resolution of social dispute and hence established the justice of revolutionary conduct. Typically, where those who are seeking to adjust the status quo are arguing from justice, this revolutionary logic will dominate. Where virtue, beauty, equality or liberty are in question, the chance of the framework itself coming under attack is slighter, though (as the case of Savanarola abundantly shows) extreme championship even of virtue can lead to the stigmatisation of the framework itself as part of the problem and can thus justify revolutionary action.

There is, however, one salient characteristic common to all genuine clashes between principles, whether peaceful or violent – viz. the discovery of a new resolution that takes its own place as part of the framework and becomes in its turn part of society's definition of the acceptable. Such clashes, in other words, 'move a civilisation on' from one resting-point to another. Where the origins even of a violent clash lie in the incompatibility of claims each of which is inherent to the civilisation, the resolution of the clash establishes a new understanding of the proper, practical balance between the conflicting arguments. Often enough the new resolutions will be long-lasting and the society will build upon them rather than quickly reversing them.

By contrast, when barbarism enters the picture, it is in principle impossible to find a lasting resolution within the framework of prior resolutions. The meaning of 'barbarism', here, is the refusal to acknowledge the values inherent in a civilisation. An advocate, for example, of prosperity who simply cannot see any merit in the claims of beauty or virtue and who consequently seeks unbridled licence to destroy that which is aesthetically and morally valuable, is seeking something which our civilisation cannot grant without damaging its own identity. The claims of beauty and virtue are inherent: even if they are wholly neglected for a period, they will not go away until and unless the civilisation is wholly replaced by barbarism – a state of affairs in which, paradoxically, prosperity is well-nigh unimaginable. As a result, wealth-barbarism is bound either to fail utterly or to succeed only briefly. And this pattern can be generalised: where the claim of true principles is entirely suppressed, there can be no resolution upon which to build. There can be no way of regarding the settlement as a new definition of the limits of the acceptable, since that which is to any civilised member of civilisation manifestly unacceptable has been perpetrated and must in due time be reversed. It is for society as it is within an individual conscience. I can pretend to myself for a period that I do not care about virtue or beauty or justice or prosperity, but I cannot keep up the pretence for very long because the truth is that I *do* care about all of those things; this is a part of what it is to be me. And so also for our society, the temporary triumph of barbarism cannot mask the fact that we collectively feel all of these claims, collectively recognise that the claims of all of them must to some degree be acknowledged and reflected in the patterns of our social life.

It is important to recognise that barbarism may be either self-interested or heroic. The heroic barbarian who is an absolute proponent of some great cause is even more dangerous than the selfish barbarian, since he may carry others more powerfully with him. The selfish barbarian is obvious to all as a destructive force, and one who over time will be driven out or be driven underground by others. Thus, for example, the Mafia, though horrible, is ultimately a parasite upon, rather than a threat to the continued existence of our civilisation. The heroic barbarian, by contrast, has an air of romance. How fine, how noble, carelessly to abandon all hope of values until now so cherished, and to fight single-mindedly *only* for justice, or virtue or whatever the particular form of heroism may demand! Savanarola is ultimately more attractive, and hence more dangerous, than Al Capone.

We, in our time, do not have to look far to find peculiarly awful and destructive examples of heroic barbarism. Nazism and Leninism are classics of the genre. Each of them affords, in its own way, a remarkable demonstration both of the destructive power of heroic barbarism and of the fate that ultimately meets such tendencies. Leninism, at first carried forward on a wave of enthusiasm for the simplicity of the disdain it showed for all the principles save equality, crippled the civilisation of half the globe for more than half a century. And still, the destruction, although wholesale at the political level and in terms of human life, was radically incomplete. The essentials of civilisation – the recognition of other principles – came gradually and with increasing force to bear upon the barbarians. Despite desperate efforts at indoctrination, the inherited conceptions of liberty, of justice, of beauty, of prosperity, so far from being totally eradicated, remained in the hearts and minds of those many millions of individuals of whose language they formed a part. Even the heroism of the Leninist barbarians could not make people forget their love of these things. In the end, the barbarians themselves lost faith in the romance of their heroism. They began to speak a language that incorporated an acknowledgement of other principles. They began, as one might say, to *let their own voices* speak their own natural language. They came to acknowledge in themselves thoughts and feelings that, as the inheritors of a civilisation, they had consciously ignored but had never wholly lost. In short, and most devastating to the barbarians, that other great principle of civilisation, truth, began to assert itself in the form of self-recognition and in the ending of the heroic propensity to lies and self-deception for the sake of a supposedly 'greater cause'. The history of Leninism is, in other words, with compelling irony the history of the explosion of the internal contradictions of a creed which attempts to deny most of the fundamentals of a civilised existence.

Nazism, though in some respects parallel, represents a different and equally archetypal pattern. Nazis were driven by their celebration of race-power to achieve and exert control over a never-endingly accumulating area of the globe. In so doing, they acquired a romantic, Nietzschean appeal. They distinguished themselves from a mere gang of self-interested thugs by legitimising their thuggery, using the authority of the state and the force of the aesthetic in oratory, the visual arts, music and, culminatingly, on the parade ground, to trumpet the glory of might. Instead of merely exploiting civilisation as self-interested parasites, they launched, like the Leninists, a direct attack upon civilisation. As with barbaric attacks from without in ages past, Nazism was repulsed. Its failure should not, however, be allowed to blind us to the fact that a heroic barbarism can prove a severe threat to the existence of civilisation and can come close to triumph. The lesson of Nazism, as of Leninism, is not so much that heroic barbarism ultimately fails, as that civilisation is continuously exposed to the danger of barbarism both from within and without, and above all to the danger of heroic barbarisms.

Barbarism is not, however, by any means the only threat to the steady continuance of civilisation. Each particular form of civilisation is also continuously exposed to threats arising from other civilisations. Any given civilised society, being a particular fragment of the kaleidoscope, has its own patterns of existence at a given moment, its own resolutions of the tensions between the various principles, its own character expressed in its own language, its morality and religion, its codes of justice, its aesthetic canons, its allocations and containments of power, its modes of practical, business-like conduct. Any other society, whether from another village, another nation or another continent, though perhaps equally recognisably civilised, will have its differences. As such, it will constitute a threat to the integrity of its neighbours. This threat may become a reality through invasion – either conscious and aggressive as in armed conquest or unconscious, gradual and peaceful as in the inter-penetration of a stronger, more vibrant civilisation with a weaker, more lethargic civilisation. Whether the threat is regarded by the members of the 'invaded' civilisation as indeed threatening or as welcome depends in part on whether the method of invasion is peaceful or war-like, in part upon whether the pace of invasion is such that it can be gradually accommodated, in part upon the extent and depth of the difference between the invading and invaded, and in part upon the self confidence and 'capability to absorb' of the invaded civilisation. In some cases, as, for example, the slight introduction of elements of Oriental civilisation into Western Europe in the early 19th century, the invasion takes the form of syncretism and is regarded as a wholly beneficial absorption. In other cases, as, for example, the conquest of Britain by the Normans or of the American Indians by Europeans, the invasion is strongly resisted and heavily obliterative. To the extent that the method, pace, character and relative self-confidence of the two civilisations permits a relatively painless absorption, the 'invasion' may enrich the invaded. But, to the extent that one civilisation is merely replaced by another, there is a net loss – a reduction in the diversity of life. One of the features of civilised life, the celebration of other civilisations, the acknowledgement of the romance of 'the distinct' would be lost altogether if – to reduce to the point of absurdity – all civilisations were to be so continuously inter-penetrative that no differences could any longer be detected.

A civilisation is thus constantly in flux, constantly exposed to danger. To the internal tensions between principles and the constant need to find resolutions, one must add the danger arising from barbaric self-interest, the even greater danger of the heroic barbarism that glorifies a single principle or a single set of principles to the near extinction of all others, and the threat of unabsorbable invasion by other civilisations. It is the presence of these dangers that makes politics a necessary part of civilised existence.

3 The Role of Politics

The essence of political action

Manifestly, politics is something that happens only within a civilised society. One cannot speak meaningfully of 'politics' in the context of a herd of buffalo, or even in the context of the subsistence-existence of Neanderthal cave dwellers. Politics is an activity carried on between inhabitants of a 'polis', an entity sufficiently civilised to have identified itself as a society and hence necessarily a sufficiently civilised society for its citizens to carry on disputes in some form other than warfare.

Within a 'polis', the inhabitants – despite being civilised – will be subject, as human beings, to the continuous attraction of unenlightened self-interest. This, not being one of the principles of civilisation but rather intrinsically a barbaric phenomenon and hence a threat to civilisation, has somehow to be contained if it is to be prevented from destroying the fabric and products of civilised life. Accordingly, the first role of politics is to provide a means of constraining self-interest where it threatens undue damage to civilised life.

Once this fundamental point is grasped, the otherwise impossibly perplexed relationship of politics to liberty becomes apparent. Liberty is itself one of the principles of civilisation. A herd of slaves, directed in every thought and deed by an unimaginably absolute and effective totalitarian tyranny, could not by any stretch of the imagination be described as living a civilised life, any more than a computer or a flock of sheep can be said to be participating in civilisation. To be a civilised person is to be a person in the full-blown sense, an individual, thinking and acting for oneself, capable not merely of automatic response but of creativity. In civilised life, individuals recognise each other as equivalent centres of self and engage with one another. Hence, each must be endowed with a liberty sufficient to *be* a centre of self, an individual creative participant in the conversation of mankind. Liberty is, in other words, as intrinsic a feature of civilisation as any other. Its claims cannot be ignored except by the barbarian. And this – given the nature of the human predicament – entails the recognition of the individual's freedom to act in his own unenlightened self-interest. Without such licence, there could be no liberty, since a continuous control over thought and deed would be required if human beings were to be prevented at every turn from engaging in pursuits dictated by their unenlightened self-interest. In an effort to prevent the barbaric pursuit of such self-interest, liberty – and hence, with crushing irony – civilised life itself, would be wholly extinguished. This, then, is the explanation of the apparent paradox (noted in Chapter 1) that both a life without liberty and a life of untramelled liberty are worthless. Both the requirement for liberty and the limits of liberty are in principle established by civilisation. If there is to be a civilised life, the individual living that life must be free to participate as a creative self in the conversation and must therefore be given wide licence; but the limits upon that licence must be such that unenlightened self interest is not permitted to destroy the fabric of the civilised society. Necessarily, if this explanation of the limits of liberty is accepted in principle, the practical consequences will be uncertain, changing, subtle and open to continuing debate. There is, here, no Mill-like simple, prescriptive formula. Rather there is the dreadful problem of attempting to judge, day by day, in the light of particular historical circumstances, whether particular constraints on self-interest will, when taken together with the rest of the circumstances, constitute a restriction on liberty so great as to begin to threaten the ability of individuals to participate creatively in the civilised conversation or whether, on the contrary, the constraints in question are required in order to prevent the clash of self-interest from posing too great a threat to the fabric of civilised life. A constraint will always to some degree have *both* effects, and there is always a need for judgement. The making of such judgements is the essence of the first role of politics in a civilised society. There is no handbook, no formula, no certain method that will replace this continuous activity of judgement. A civilised society can balance the civilised requirement for liberty against the need to protect civilisation from the clash of freely expressed self-interest only through contingent political decisions based on uncertain judgements about the often far-flung effects of intangibles.

The setting of appropriate limits to liberty and hence to the play and clash of self-interest would not, however, be a sufficient condition for civilised life even if it could be permanently and perfectly achieved. The tensions between the principles of civilisation have also to be resolved in practical, concrete situations. The achievement of such resolutions is the second role of politics. Seen from this point of view, politics is the arena in which the members of a civilised society constantly readjust the shape of society in response to the claims of the various principles, allowing first one and then another to exert its influence so that when the society seems at any given moment to have been distorted by the exaggerated influence of one principle, it is restored to appropriateness by alterations in response to the claim of an opposing principle.

Once this role of politics is understood, various mysteries are resolved. The relation of politics to equality, for example, becomes clear. Every potential participant in a civilisation is just that – a potential participant. Part of what it is to be civilised is to recognise that status of participation: without such recognition, it is impossible for one individual to engage with another in a civilised discourse and civilised practice. This recognition, in itself, gives rise to the call for a form of equality: an equal right to participate. But such engagement requires also, beyond mutual recognition, the ability of each participant to engage. It requires the endowment of each individual participant with sufficient leisure and sufficient education to play a part as fully as that participant's talents and character will permit. In short, a thoroughly civilised life depends, not indeed upon some abstractly idealised and comprehensive equality, but upon the absence of such inequalities as would deprive some potential participants of the ability to participate. In a society where there is even moderate wealth, sufficient to support participation in the civilisation by the broad mass of the population, there will be a pull to equality arising from the desire to see such universal or near-universal participation in civilised discourse. At the same time, however, if comprehensive equality becomes an over-riding goal, the demands of beauty, prosperity, virtue, justice, liberty and so forth will be unduly neglected, and civilisation, so far from gaining, will lose. Accordingly, if one of the prime roles of politics is to reconcile the principles in such a way as to permit the flourishing of a civilisation, politics will need to aim, not at equality at all costs but at the eradication, so far as feasible within the constraints imposed by the economy, of such inequalities as prevent or diminish the ability of particular individuals to participate in civilised life; and politics will need to balance this against the requirement to attend adequately to the substantive achievements of civilised life (beauty, truth, virtue) and to the instrumental requirements of civilisation (prosperity, justice, liberty).

What is true of equality is true also of the other principles. In its role as a provider of concrete resolutions between the principles, politics can never be the ultimate partisan of one or the other. It can be only temporarily the partisan of whichever principle at a given time has come, or has come to be seen, to have too little influence over the shape of the society. Instead of any one of the desiderata identified in Chapter I being 'the aim of politics', each desideratum takes it place as one of the principles to which politics may attend at any given time, in pursuit of the reformation (and through reformation, preservation) of the fabric of the civilisation.

The setting of civilised limits to liberty and self-interest and the continuous reformation of society through the achievement of particular resolutions of the tensions between the principles inherent in that society's civilisation may seem to constitute a sufficiently significant role for politics. But even these tasks do not constitute a complete description of what politics has to do if it is to preserve civilisation. Both the threats of barbarism from without and the threats of invasion of the civilisation by other civilisations have also to be countered. Seen in this light, politics is an organised activity – a method of bringing together those within the civilised society so that they can together defend themselves, at times by peaceful means, at other times if necessary by force, against such external threats. This is not to say that the activity of international policing or fighting is in itself directly political; it is, rather, to say that, in and through its politics, a civilised society establishes for itself the means by which it will defend itself. 'Foreign policy' in its widest sense is as much a part of politics as is a 'domestic' concern with the limits of liberty or the resolution of tensions between the principles. In 'foreign policy' as much as in the field of 'domestic policy', politics has the role of defending the residents of the civilised society against that which may threaten the continued flourishing or even, ultimately, the very survival of their civilisation.

The thesis advanced in this book is, in short, that the proper, ultimate purpose of politics is not the pursuit of any one of the aims identified in Chapter I, but rather the continuously changing identification within a civilisation of effective, practical responses to the clashes of self-interest, the tensions between the principles inherent to the civilisation and the threats from without, to the point where the civilisation of that society is continuously protected from those dangers. My claim is that politics is – or at least should be –

the servant of civilisation. It remains, however, to illustrate the particular nature of the service that it performs – what *kind* of servant it is, and how it differs from the other principal servants of civilisation.

Politics and law

The first and most obvious coadjutor of politics is law. Like politics, law sets limits on liberty and hence on the clash of unenlightened self-interest. Like politics, too, it embodies, in its verdicts and adjudications, resolutions of the tensions between the principles of a civilisation. What then is the difference – if any – between politics and law? First, law in a civilised society is a result whereas politics is a cause: the law, either explicitly as statute or code, or implicitly as precedent, embodies the resolutions derived from political discussion. Second, law is a system founded on constrained rules of argument whereas political argument is a game without frontiers. Third, the formation and application of law depends upon procedures whose criterion is legitimacy, whereas politics has as its criterion, desirability. These three ostensibly distinct points are in fact no more than aspects of the same fundamental point. In politics, the members of a civilised society debate the means of preserving and enhancing their civilisation; this is a substantive discussion, whose character will alter infinitely with an infinite range of concrete circumstances, as the proponents of differing principles and differing interests meet and interpret those circumstances; but in the course of this unending discussion it is, if not absolutely necessary, at least massively convenient to establish certain, necessarily temporary 'arrests' or halting-points by enshrining certain resolutions in law, thus removing them temporarily from substantive discussion. True, every legal judgement is in some sense (as it has become fashionable to assert) a political judgement since it sets or at least recognises a limitation or resolution. Nevertheless, the *raison d'être* of legal judgement is that it is distinct from political judgement. It is a judgement to be made following constrained procedures and constrained forms of argument, against the background of settled rules, where the criterion of correctness is not the desirability of the individual outcome but the legitimacy of the outcome in terms of those constraints and rules. Law is, in other words, the means whereby politics makes it possible for the civilisation to take much as a 'given' and to debate only a little, in the hope that the discussion can thereby be contained in scope and be itself civilised in form.

Nowhere is this relationship between civilised politics and law better seen than in the sphere of constitutional law – the type of law that governs political discussion itself. Manifestly, a constitution cannot establish either its own desirability or the desirability of any substantive political outcome. The constitution is therefore continuously open to political challenge on the grounds that the procedures laid down by it somehow fail to provide an adequate framework for the contingent resolution of the tensions within a civilisation, the setting of limits to licence, or the establishment of defence against external threats. But the constitution, being a temporary 'arrest' of the political process, nevertheless sets a framework of procedure and establishes a measure of legitimacy which, if adhered to, helps to prevent politics itself from becoming an uncivilised activity. This is the archetypal resolution in the sense that politics, here, delivers law which results in a particular constitution, is enabled by that deliverance to conduct itself in a civilised fashion and – as part of that conduct – is nevertheless able not only to continue debating the substantive issues which arise from the tensions between the various principles of the civilisation but also to offer from time to time a critique of the constitution itself. That is a paradigm for the political resolution of the tensions within a civilised society progressively encoded in and continuously assisted by law – providing civilised 'arrests' of the political process, though not, in a world of changing particulars, arrests that can ever be in any sense 'final'.

It is nearly inconceivable that there could be a civilisation in which politics was conducted without the benefit of such 'arrests' provided by legal codification. In the absence, at any given moment, of a settled framework of rules and procedures against which, and in the light of which, actions can be tested relatively uncontroversially for legitimacy as opposed to desirability, the political game without frontiers would all too easily lose its character as a peaceful pastime of civilised disputants and turn to strife or suppression of strife – a barbaric rather than a civilised outcome. Politics cannot, in other words, for any practical purpose be expected to fulfil its role as defender of civilisation except in the context of law – with each political adjustment temporarily arrested in a legal codification that itself becomes both a constraint on, and a possible target for, subsequent criticism by politics. This does not imply that politics in a civilisation will always be wholly law-abiding, since it is feasible – even if the particular examples are open to contention – that there should be a law or a regime acting within the law, thought to be so deleterious to the survival of the civilisation that action against the law is seen as necessary to restore the balance. But here we enter the realm of transcendent politics discussed in Chapter 6. Normal politics – politics, that is, in the context of a society which is fundamentally civilised – must, if it is to advance the cause of that civilisation, carry with it the benefits of its past by taking as its starting point the law which embodies the results of that past. This, indeed, is the *definition* of 'normal' politics, that it moves from past to future guided by the legal monuments of the past and encoding its results in the legal monuments of the future. In other words, the normal situation of politics in a civilisation is to have the law both as its frame of reference and as its transient, formal object – the frame of reference being the existing law, and the formal object being the creation of new law in which to embody new resolutions that are regarded as substantively desirable.

We can, then, regard politics as a spider that lives in and gradually amends a web of laws sufficiently strong to hold together in appropriate relationships the various principles of civilisation and the many conflicting self-interests within a civilised society. And in this image, we capture Burke's conception of the settled and historically evolved arrangements of society as an inheritance which reconciles the conflicting passions of mankind in a manner far superior to anything that can be achieved by a single act of 'rational' planning. To conceive politics as the servant of civilisation, and as a servant that acts through the encoding in law of amendments to law which resolve continuously the inherent tensions of the civilisation, is inevitably to take a Burkean, accumulative view of politics. Neither the civilisation itself, nor the laws in which the resolutions that hold it together, are created (or, if destroyed, re-created) in a trice, but must rather be constructed laboriously over time. Inevitably, as events march on, much of the reason for each element of the construction will subsequently be forgotten, only to be remembered once a revision alters the shape of the web and some tension, previously ignored as a result of having been resolved, again becomes apparent. It follows that each political amendment in a law – even if seen at the time as critically necessary to resolving a particular tension – must be undertaken with hesitation, lest it undo some good work previously undertaken. The view of politics as the instrument for resolving – through legal amendment – tensions within the civilisation is thus necessarily one which entails an evolutionary rather than a revolutionary attitude to change.

The close involvement of politics in the law – the close involvement of the spider in its web – can from time to time, make it nearly impossible to apply the formal distinctions between legal and political decision-making. In constitutional courts (a prime example in the present day being the European Court of Justice) the key distinction between the legal criterion of the procedurally determined legitimacy and the political criterion of the desirability of outcome is frequently obscured. It then becomes impossible to say whether such a court is a legal or a political institution. And if such a situation were to become the norm, as some writers have held it, or perhaps wished it to be, then the notion of law as something distinct from politics would break down.

There would no longer be any 'arrests' in the political process to constrain the otherwise limitless game without frontiers, and we would lose the civilising influence which such constraint has on politics itself. Civilisation is thus dependent not only on the close involvement of politics with law but also, and equally, upon the preservation of the distinction between legal and political modes of action. It is in their distinct roles, and in these roles alone, that politics and law can serve civilisation effectively by creating a web of resolution that holds a civilised society together.

Politics and strife

The distinction between politics and strife is entirely different in character from that between politics and law. In the case of politics and strife, we are dealing not with closely related and mutually supportive items but with opposites, wholly exclusive of one another. Politics is not possible until and unless the sword has given way to the ploughshare – because political activity consists in the use of language rather than in the use of violence to achieve resolution. The proposition that politics is in essence peaceable may at first glance appear contentious or implausible. Are there not, after all, instances of elections and other clearly 'political' events being accompanied by considerable violence? Is not bloody revolution itself a form of politics just as warfare is, famously, a form of foreign policy? Such questions prompt the view, perhaps widely shared, that violence aimed at achieving social change is politics by other means. But that view – for all its apparent plausibility – is in fact no more than a confusion, as can been seen by considering the case of a pair of cavemen who fight over the fire. This *can* of course be described as a system of politics, on the grounds that anything *can* be described by any name, but to apply such a description would be to obscure rather than to illuminate. In the full-blooded sense of the word, such an inarticulate fight between cavemen can no more be described as an engagement in politics than can a fight between a pair of dogs over a bone. What distinguishes politics from mere strife is, first, the fact that it is regularised disagreement – disagreement within the context of rules or at least conventions; and, second, that it is articulated disagreement. Of course, articulate political debate may be *accompanied* by violence: but to the extent that it is so accompanied, its political character is compromised, and if it becomes *merely* violent, its political character is wholly lost.

There is no question, here, of quibbling about words. Rather, the point is to preserve a useful concept. If we did not have the idea of politics as a distinctive, articulate, rule-based activity, separate from violence, we would need to invent it. The purpose of describing a disagreement as 'political' is precisely to denote it as something articulate and essentially distinct from violence – something essentially civilised. There is, in other words, a deep *formal* connection between politics and civilisation. Just as language, either shared or translated, is critical to the establishment and survival of anything recognisable as a civilisation, so the use of language to debate issues within a civilisation is critical to the pursuit of anything recognisable as political. Just as a framework of commonly accepted convention is fundamental to anything recognisable as a civilisation, so an accepted framework of political debate is fundamental to anything recognisable as politics. Just as a degree of social peace is critical to anything recognisable as a civilisation, so a degree of peaceful exchange of ideas is fundamental to anything recognisable as politics. Consideration of the distinction between politics and strife leads, in short, to the observation that the fundamental pre-requisites of civilisation are at the same time the fundamental pre-requisites of politics.

The distinction between politics and strife – made, for example, in the frequently quoted observation that 'there must be a political rather than a military solution' – is illuminated by the relationship between politics and symbolism. In strife – at its ultimate, in 'military solutions' – the aim of each side consists in achieving goals by forcing the other at gunpoint to conform to the will of the victor: winning means grabbing or repelling. In politics, by contrast, the grabbing or repelling takes the form of what Sartre refers to as 'magic': the actors engage in purely symbolic acts – speaking, writing, voting – which *indicate* the will but do not in themselves enforce it. The translation of the magic into achievement occurs only through convention and rule. The speaking and writing leads under convention or rule to voting, and the voting by rule leads to resolutions which are themselves by rule enforceable. True, force lurks behind, as an ever-present threat; but it is to be invoked only in the enforcement of what is conventionally or by explicit rule accepted as the outcome of the 'magic' or symbolic acts. Both the symbolic acts themselves and the conventions or rules that lead to their interpretation and enforceability are, of course, intrinsically articulate: rules and symbolic acts – unlike acts of violence –

can exist only if articulated. Hence, they can exist only against the background of a framework of conventions and common acceptances – in short, against the framework of a civilisation. One can say, therefore, that in politics, as opposed to mere strife, force is *tamed* by the magic of symbolic acts and representations – a form of magic which is possible only in a civilisation. In this sense, politics consists of the civilising of force itself.

Politics is, then, linked to civilisation not only by the fact that it, unlike strife, is itself civilised but also by the fact that, unlike strife, it is civilis*ing*. In politics, and in the legal framework with which politics is intertwined, the tensions of a civilisation are not only resolved but also resolved in a way that eliminates the barbarism of strife and thus protects the civilisation from types of revolution which pose a threat to its continuance. Persons who are members of a society in which politics is practised in place of strife are *ipso facto* members of a civilised society, and persons who find themselves in a place in which strife replaces politics are, to the extent of that substitution, *ipso facto* in a condition approaching barbarism, and hence in a condition which cannot be recognised as fully 'social'.

Politics, oratory and argument

The *character* of the symbolic acts involved in politics is also important. At the first level of approximation, this character can be described as 'persuasion'. To engage in political action is to make an utterance that seeks to *persuade*. There are, of course, such things as political analysis, political commentary and political history; but to the extent that those engaging in such activities are doing something other than to persuade, they cannot be said to be engaging in political action itself. A political utterance is one intending to induce change in a course of action, or is part of a strategy aimed at such a result – and this, in the absence of force, can occur only through persuasion.

It is not, however, sufficient to identify politics with the act of persuasion. Beyond this first level of approximation, at least two distinct species of persuasion can be discerned, each with its own and very different place in politics. These two species of persuasion can be captured by two political phrases, each well known in history: 'we will fight them on the beaches' and 'no taxation without representation'.

The difference between these two phrases can be brought out by considering how far each can be taken literally. Would someone be said to have recognised the force and intention of 'we will fight them on the beaches' if he began to challenge the *accuracy* of the statement? Was it really beaches that would be an appropriate place to do the fighting as opposed to the sand dunes or the ditches? One might, of course, ask such a question as an elaborate kind of joke, but if one asked it in any other spirit one would be rightly accused of having missed the point – not, of course, the literal meaning of the phrase as a phrase, but the *point* in the sense of the *purpose* of the utterance. In using the phrase, Churchill did not intend to announce a novel military strategy, to warn the enemy of the exact location of the Home Guard, or to argue that beaches were on military grounds the best possible places for fighting on. Rather, he intended his audience to intimate a spirit of defiance. The form of the utterance is metaphoric and its aim oratorical: it seeks to persuade not through argument but through encouragement, emotional charge, example. 'No taxation without representation', by contrast, though a banner under which to sail, is nevertheless an argument to be taken literally. It means exactly what it says. In short form, admittedly, but resonantly and clearly enough it makes the argument that – to spell it out more pedantically – 'it is not fair or appropriate that certain persons should bear the burden of taxation by the state without having the opportunity to influence the scale of that burden and the use to which those collective taxes are put'. In the concision of the phrase, there is an element of the oratorical – but in the concision only. With an expansion that strips the phrase of its concision and hence of its rhetorical force, the statement, unlike 'we will fight them on the beaches', stands up as a statement of policy and as an appeal to reason.

Here, then, are two distinct forms of political persuasion – oratory and argument. Both have a role in enabling politics to affect action without the use of force. But they establish different relationships between the persuader and the persuaded and have different effects within the society in which they are employed. From the point of view of the civilisation, argument – if genuinely uncharged by oratory – is safe but weak, whereas oratory is strong but dangerous. Argument seeks to persuade by moving from propositions accepted by the listener to propositions not yet entertained (or if entertained not yet accepted): it seeks to achieve this transition through the medium of an accepted logic. It relies, therefore, upon dispassionate and easily changeable acceptances. The introduction of a new proposition, or the application of a further accepted logic, may alter or remove the force of an argument. Since such introductions and applications are persistently available to the enquiring mind educated in a civilisation, the force of argument is always tenuous. But for the same reason, argument on its own poses little danger to the civilisation. Those hearing it and accepting it cannot easily be moved by it to discard the common practices and shared values that are constitutive of the civilisation, since it is upon such shared practices that the force of the argument itself explicitly rests: barbarians cannot argue. Oratory, by contrast, seeks to persuade by the creation of a mood – a mood that can engender distrust or dislike, without dispassionate consideration, or even in the face of opposition from the conclusions of dispassionate consideration. Oratory operates, in other words, by suspension of the logically critical faculties through the presentation to the mind of images, rhythm, echoes, memories and half-memories, hopes and fears sufficiently strong to lead, without the mediation of investigation, to action. In this immediacy lies the strength of oratory: its capacity to move masses and hence to move mountains. In the immediacy, too, lies the danger that oratory poses for civilisation. True, oratory itself as much as argument depends upon the common acceptances – for example, of language and meaning – and is hence at root a civilised phenomenon. But, in the mood of the moment, those stirred by oratory can be brought to reject or to forget large parts of the shared inheritance of practice and value – can be brought to see as inevitable, and immediately to indulge in, acts that lay waste to or fly in the face of important aspects of the civilisation itself.

There is more to be said about the difference between argument and oratory in the course of differentiating between better and worse forms of politics. But for the present it is enough to know that the two forms of political persuasion both have their place in helping politics to fulfil its roles of assisting the organisation of a civilised society to expel external threats and of bringing about, without warfare or civil strife, shifts in the kaleidoscopic patterns of the civilisation itself – shifts which are at once constituted by and constitutive of new accommodations between the conflicting interests and the conflicting principles inherent to a civilised society.

Politics as civilisation in the service of itself

This, then, *is* politics. It is an activity: (1) in which civilised people find reconciliations between opposing principles within the civilisation through a continuous sequence of reformation of their society; (2) in which civilised people accommodate conflicting self-interests and thereby set for themselves limits to their own liberties, combining sufficient freedom with sufficient constraint to permit the continuance of the civilisation; and (3) in which civilised people decide how to deal with what are, or may be, external threats to their survival as a civilisation. Though not itself constrained by the rules of legal argument, it is an activity within which each act is both itself recognised as conditioned by a pre-existing framework of law and has as its formal object a change in or a continuance of that legal framework. It is in essence a peaceful activity – one in which change is effected not through force but through the magic of symbolic acts (such as voting) whose role and results are codified in law, as well as through the more direct symbolic act of persuasive speech in the form of oratory or argument or both.

Seen in this light it becomes clear how far politics and civilisation are mutually inter-penetrative. Without a setting recognisable as civilisation, there can be no politics. Without a sphere of activity recognisable as political, there can be no civilised society. Each depends on the other – because politics *is* civilisation's civilised method of preserving itself. Politics is, in other words, civilisation in the service of itself. And politics cannot have, in the human world, any higher or more ultimate aim than this, since there can be nothing more valuable on earth than the protection of that which is, on earth, the source of value.

II The Types of Political Action

4 Politics as a
Visionary Science

Means and ends

The description of politics as civilisation in the service of
itself is cautiously optimistic: it is a description of what politics can be and should be, not of what it automatically in
practice becomes. Politics can also be, and all too often has
been, something quite else: a destructive activity which tends
to threaten rather than to preserve civilisation. Politics, like
eating, is intrinsically valuable; but like eating it can be dangerous if wrongly conducted; and like eating it can go wrong
for either of two reasons – the wrong objects or the wrong
methods.

In the history of political philosophy a great deal more
attention has been paid to ends than means. But, if the ultimate, proper aim of politics is the preservation of civilisation,
then the means by which politics is carried on become at
least as important, from the point of view of its capacity to
achieve the ultimate end, as are the transient aims with which
its participants may at a given time and place be preoccupied.

The failure to recognise this point is in fact the first, and
perhaps the most important, mark of politics in its destructive mode. In forms of politics that tend to threaten rather
than preserve civilisation, there is typically concern with
ends (i.e. transient, relatively immediate ends such as the

enactment of a particular law or the alteration of a particular policy) rather than with the means by which these transient aims are to be achieved. Such concern with ends rather than means can be described as myopic, since it derives from and at the same time reinforces a blindness to the more general effects of employing specific means on a specific occasion. 'The end I have in mind is noble; if I employ uncivilised means to attain it, civilisation will nevertheless benefit from the nobility of the achievement' is a statement which, within its bald and apparently robust simplicity, conceals almost all the short sightedness that mankind is capable of. The fabric of a civilised society – the multitude of accommodations so far reached and enacted in the laws and conventions that govern its civil discourse – is, of course, much affected by the means that participants in its politics adopt. Each time that the framework of law and convention is challenged, or even that a precedent is set for its later challenge, the validity and continuance of that framework is itself much in question. A politics that, in its pursuit of transient aims, regards means as unimportant will come sooner rather than later to disregard, and hence to encourage a universal disregard for established practice, law and tradition, as items supposedly insignificant compared to the overwhelming importance of a particular end.

The doctrine that means matter as much as ends in politics may, at some abstract level, be regarded as obvious. In practice, however, even in the most politically sophisticated societies on earth, it is as much honoured in the breach as in the observance. The 'requirements' of the 'media' and of 'political activity' of various types, give rise all too frequently to forms of political action which are bound to have a cumulatively corrosive effect on the civilisation. I am not speaking here simply of illegality, venality, scandal, abuse – behaviour which is in practice easy to identify and control. More insidious by far are the subtler abuses: the use of *ad hominem* attack to undercut a strong argument; the use of oratory not to persuade an audience of points that might otherwise, and in a calmer mood, be presented to their intelligence as arguments but instead to lure them into acceptance of positions which, on reflection, they would not wish to have taken up; the discussion of politics as if it were 'obviously' or 'always' a cynical endeavour (a pestilential form of narrow stupidity posing as high sophistication, often encountered in the 'highbrow' media); and the fulfilment in practice of such narrow cynicism through the use of glib phrases, half-truths, partisan distortion, debating tricks and the rest of the panoply of demagoguery and chat show demagoguery. These and a dozen other low ways of conducting and talking about politics are to be found not only in benighted societies where politics has almost stifled the civilisation it is meant to preserve but also in our own 'advanced' 'liberal' societies, where we pride ourselves not only on the richness of our civilisation but also on the civilised manners of our political life.

But the position is far worse in societies in which political means are truly subordinated to political ends. The claim of revolutionaries and tyrants that the end justifies the means has in our times all too often made politics a foe rather than a friend of civilisation. Out of what is, alas, a wealth of recent examples, the Chinese 'cultural revolution' – a supreme instance at once of revolution and of tyranny – illustrates the point. Even if there had been any merit in the goals which Mao and his henchmen sought to promote, the means by which these goals were pursued made the pursuit itself one of the most dangerous enemies of civilisation yet seen on the face of the earth. It would hardly be an exaggeration to say that the ends of political action become an irrelevance when the means involve a conscious attack on a rich and ancient civilisation through the displacement of persons, the destruction of the physical heritage and the rejection and elimination of every moral convention hitherto enshrined in that society's practices and beliefs. Where political method is sufficiently barbaric, civilisation has nothing to gain and much to lose from politics.

Rationalism and millenarianism: the politics of the absolute

The doctrine that the means are justified by the end is espoused by rationalists and millenarians – for whom the rationally deducible or mystically intimated end has absolute rather than merely transient validity and the means are therefore unimportant.

Beyond justifying all means, however, the politics of the absolute has the further effect of encouraging in its proponents a certain view of other participants in politics which poses a separate and almost equally dangerous threat to civilisation. For a politician who believes that, through science or vision or some combination of these powers, he can deduce or interpret for mankind the ultimate end of man beyond the mere sustenance of a happenstance civilisation, it follows that other, lesser mortals not able to follow the deduction or deprived of a share in the vision are just that – stupid or deprived, and hence wholly to be ignored and despised. It follows also that the visionary in politics believes that there is no merit whatsoever in a political method that accommodates or reconciles existing projects. So far from recognising each of his opponents as a participant in the conversion of the civilisation, the proponent of the politics of the absolute sees all of his opponents, together with their prejudices and concerns, only as a nuisance to be either ignored or eliminated.

The politics of the absolute – the opinion that political action can identify and aim towards some ultimate goal for man beyond the sustenance of civilisation – is therefore wholly inconsistent with the idea of politics as an activity whose ultimate proper aim is the preservation of civilisation through achievement of reconciliation between conflicting principles and conflicting self-interests. The proponent of the politics of the absolute sees neither the validity of resolution as an aim in itself, nor the *prima facie* legitimacy of the concerns expressed by others who are promoting either their interests or particular principles. He is, therefore, in no position to recognise the potential equivalence of opposites (the potential equivalence of himself and his opponent) or to attend to the points put forward by others. As a result, he stands not the slightest chance of achieving over however long a period the resolution of opposing trends. Ultimately, indeed, the politician of the absolute is not a politician at all, since his politics is not so much a form of politics as a form of (open or covert) warfare – an attempt to force, by the use of whatever means may be necessary, all other members of the society to conform to a certain pattern of activity on the grounds that such a pattern will lead to the absolute that he identifies as desirable. It becomes, in the extreme, practically impossible to distinguish the violence perpetrated in the name of such absolutes from the violence of a barbaric invader, and it becomes virtually as meaningless to describe as political such absolutist violence (for example, the violence of the Nazis in Germany) as it would be to speak of the 'politics' of Genghis Khan.

Not the end itself but the conception of the end

It is important to notice that what distinguishes the politics of the absolute is not the particular end at which it aims, but rather the conception that it has of the end and of the relation of the end to the world. Each absolutist may have an aim utterly different from – and typically opposing – the aims of many or all of the other absolutists. What joins together all absolutists is thus emphatically not a joint or shared aim but rather the view, taken by them all, that their particular aims, so far from constituting merely transient aims to be incorporated within the general framework of the civilisation, are ultimate and over-riding. The absolutist may, of course, be a straightforward barbarian in the sense of elevating his own self-interest to the level of an absolute end; but he may equally be a sophisticate, apparently devoted to one or more of the principles of civilisation itself. Savanarola (even assuming him to have been as pure and selfless a proponent of virtue as his supporters claimed) nevertheless, in his absolutism posed as much danger to civilisation as any villain.

Out of the absolutist's conception of his ends comes his

rationalism – his sense that his pursuit can be followed with scientific rigour. This is as true of the visionary or millenarian form of absolutism as of the fully rationalised or deduced form. Regardless of whether a person believes that the absolute validity of his chosen end derives from visionary intimation or from rational deduction, if he believes himself to have knowledge of the ultimate end, he needs only to work out what requires to be done to achieve that end (in total disregard of all other constraints) and then follow that policy. The politics of the absolute thereby becomes, in contrast to civilised politics, 'easy'. Such politics is not constrained by the difficulties and hesitations necessarily imposed upon those who recognise the substantive force of many opposing principles. Nor is it constrained by the need to adopt means that fall within the pre-existing norms of the civilised society. The lure, the excitement and the sense of romantic liberation so often associated with the politics of the absolute lies precisely in this simplicity, this lack of constraint. In the politics of the absolute, just as in love, or creative art, or any great work, the apparently overwhelming importance of the present pursuit liberates the actor from petty cares. In absolute politics both leader and led conceive of themselves as engaged in something at once so important and (in its importance) so obviously correct that they experience – so we are told – a sense of liberation and aesthetic enjoyment. The remark in the diary of Lenin's wife that she had no idea the revolution would be so beautiful expresses in a single phrase the typical disregard (apparently genuinely complete) of all the suffering and destruction entailed by the act of revolution and hence the capacity to revel in the romantic simplicities of the act itself: the massed ranks moving in torch-lit procession, the skies illuminated by the fires burning in the palaces, the magnificent, obvious, rigorous inevitability of it all.

The absence of arguments against the visionary

It is one thing to point out the danger for civilisation posed by the politics of the absolute, quite another to provide a coherent argument against such absolutism. Whether such an argument can indeed be provided is a real issue. Is there any basis upon which one can argue convincingly for the superiority of civilisation over any one of the principles that exist within it?

Much importance, here, attaches to the sense in which one understands the term 'argument'. It is relatively easy to marshal reasons, convincing to a person who is already happily attached to civilisation, why the absolutist is mistaken. One has merely to point out the extent to which the absolutist – in his passionate enthusiasm for one of the principles – excludes the rest. This is the argument advanced in the first part of this book on the supposition that its readers will be civilised persons and hence persons who place some emphasis on all the principles in our civilisation. But there is little or no point in advancing such an argument against the absolutist himself, since for him it is a mantra rather than an argument. His assertion is that the end to which he attaches supreme importance is ultimate rather than in any sense transient; the recitation of other ends, therefore, seems to him merely incantatory and void. He knows already that he is sacrificing things to which other people attach importance:

his claim is precisely that they are wrong to do so and he is not impressed by being reminded that they disagree with him.

True, some headway might be made against a rational absolutist of certain kinds on grounds of coherence: for example, an absolute proponent of justice might be convinced to take some account of virtue on the argument that justice itself conceptually implies an attachment to virtue, since justice has to do with ensuring that people receive what they deserve, and virtue is at least one of the bases of being deserving. Similarly, one might be able to persuade an absolute proponent of virtue that justice had at least some absolute weight, on the grounds that exhibiting justice is clearly one of the virtues. Perhaps, on a different plane, one might also convince absolutists of a certain kind of the existence of relevant practical rather than conceptual implications – for example, of the dependence of certain kinds of beauty upon certain kinds of prosperity. But there is no reason to suppose that, even if these arguments can be made convincingly in some cases, this would be true in all cases. On the contrary, it seems clear that there is little, if any, implication between, say, beauty and justice: and at a practical level these two principles seem frequently to be opposed. Indeed, the encounter between beauty and justice is one of the great hidden conflicts of history; with astonishing frequency beauty has been preserved or achieved at the expense of what most of us today at any rate think of as just treatment of the losers. From the slavery that built the Parthenon or the pyramids, through the enclosures and primogeniture that sustained the great English country houses, to the planning restrictions and hidden subsidies that protect the peace of the countryside against the invasion of the urban masses, the centuries have witnessed repeatedly, in the changing idiom of each generation, a sacrifice of a fair distribution of rights in favour of the preservation and creation of the beautiful. In this conflict, there is no reason to suppose the possibility of *arguing* against either the absolutist proponent of beauty or the absolutist proponent of justice.

The problem is not that the absolutist has a cast-iron argument to back his claim. It is, rather, that the basis for rational discourse between the absolutist and the proponent of civilisation is largely missing. In some cases, the absolutist may *claim* to have 'logic on his side'. But even where this claim is at its strongest (e.g. in relation to virtue, a concept which, as a matter of its internal logic, does claim for itself an imperative and ultimate character), the claim is in truth weak, since even where it is a fact that the concept proposed by the absolutist claims for itself absolute superiority, this does not establish the legitimacy of that claim. And in some cases (e.g. beauty, prosperity or equality) there is not even the appearance of such a logic in the concept itself. Debate is, therefore, generally futile as between absolutists of different persuasions or between the proponents of civilisation and absolutists of any persuasion. Instead of rational discourse, we have at best an elegantly disguised shouting match and at worst outright warfare. To say that the encounter between absolutists and the proponents of civilisation collapses quickly into an assertion of contradictory preferences is not to say that this is a matter of 'mere preference'. When one person likes lamb chops and another likes pork chops, there are plenty of ways of accommodating both preferences, and nothing very deep is at stake: one might say that it is a matter of preference because it does not much matter. In the dispute between the absolutist and the proponent of civilisation, on the contrary, something very deep is at stake – the nature and aim of human society. We may say, in this case, that it is a matter of preference because it matters so much. Civilisation is fundamental; it forms, for its adherents, the foundation of value; those absolutists who reject it must accordingly be seen as barbarians – an enemy against whom neither civilised method nor arguments premissed on civilisation can be employed and who must be either ignored, or contained or defeated by force.

In sum, the politics of the absolute ceases to be in the ordinary sense political, not only because it ceases to attend to the methods that distinguish it from strife, but also because its substance cannot be debated in a truly political fashion. It leads inevitably and rapidly to overt or covert warfare with all who oppose it and thus becomes, rather than a friend or servant of civilisation, a radical, barbaric foe.

5 Politics as a Constructive Art

A practical politics

The dangers of political absolutism, if regarded as a photographic negative, illustrate by direct contradiction the positive features that are required to make politics a true servant of civilisation.

The starting-point for a politics that is, from the point of view of civilisation, constructive, is the recognition that it must be in the full sense a political politics – a politics that identifies itself as something wholly different from strife. This single and apparently uncontroversial conception contains a welter of implications. In the first place, it implies the recognition of the potential equivalence of opposing views. No matter what interest or principle a proponent of a practical politics may at a given moment be representing, he will recognise the legitimacy and hence arguability of the position of a political opponent who is representing a different interest or principle. For, without this acknowledgement of at least potential equivalence, the debate will collapse into strife as fast as any attempt to debate with an absolutist.

The establishment of a politics which consists of debate rather than strife, however, depends upon more than merely the mutual recognition of potentially equivalent positions. It depends also upon: a willingness to reach an accommodation; a recognition that such accommodations are contingent, and can never represent final resolutions since they may be challenged by the representatives of other principles or interests in changed circumstances; the acknowledgement that, in both the accommodation and the debate itself, civilised methods not involving strife are to be employed; a consequent willingness to abide by the framework of established practices and laws which prevail in a civilised society; and the understanding that these practices and laws are ultimately of more significance than the particular issue at hand. The proponent of a practical politics is able to make his politics an example of civilisation in the service of itself precisely because, in complete contradiction to the absolutist, he fully accepts that his ends are transient and that they are always less important than the means employed to achieve them.

It is important to be clear that the distinction between the politics of the absolute and a practical politics is not in the slightest degree equivalent to a distinction between 'idealism' and pragmatic, world-weary, cynical opportunism. True, the proponent of a truly political politics will be willing, unlike the absolutist, to abandon the search for a complete acceptance of his position; he will be willing to accept accommodations, and to abide by the established conventions and rules even when they are disadvantageous to his case. But these attitudes arise from his own absolute – the absolute requirement that, come what transient goals there may, civilisation has to be preserved. One does not, in other words, have to be an absolutist (which is to say, a barbarian) in order to be an 'idealist' or a person of principle: the ultimate 'ideal' or principle for which one strives in the case of a truly political pol-

itics exists as fully as it does for the absolutist; it is merely subtler, being at one remove from the immediate scene of
action, and it typically impinges upon that scene at least
partly in what Oakeshott called an adverbial mode – as a set
of negative constraints upon action rather than as a positive
attempt to direct action. Whether the absolutist or the proponent of a practical politics is actually an 'idealist' or a mere
opportunist will depend not on the way in which he con-
ducts his politics but on his motive. If either the absolute goal
of the absolutist or the transient goal of a practical politician
is self-interest, then we have an example of opportunism – in
the one case, barbaric opportunism, unconstrained by the
existing framework of civilisation; in the other case, civilised
opportunism constrained by acknowledgement of the
framework and the constraints it imposes. If, however, the
absolute goal of the absolutist or the transient goal of the
proponent of a practical politics is the representation of a
genuine principle, then we have a case of 'idealism'. In the
first instance, barbaric idealism which threatens the continuance of the civilisation despite its moral nobility; in the
second circumstance, a civilised idealism qualified by the
acknowledgement of the transience of the aim and of the
over-riding significance of the civilisation. Nobility of
motive must, in other words, be distinguished from the type
of politics espoused. When it comes to politics, either noble
motives or base motives can be entertained by barbarians or
by civilised persons. It is critical to the survival of the civilisation that society should be able to distinguish barbaric
nobility from civilised nobility and barbaric opportunism
from civilised opportunism. From the point of view of a

moral judgement on the person concerned, it is the distinction between nobility and opportunism that counts. From the point of view of deciding with whom to argue and with whom to fight, the distinction that counts is that between the barbarian, with whom one must fight, and the civilised operator, with whom one must argue.

Constructive politics as a sense of history

In order to be truly political – that is, *inter alia*, to avoid a descent into strife – constructive political action has to take the form of debate within the pre-established framework of practice and law. So much is obvious. Not so obvious are the limits, if any, on the type of debate or on the techniques and aims of debate. If actual warfare is avoided, and the action taken is in conformity with the dictates of the established framework, is all, from the point of view of civilisation, well? Frequently enough, and perhaps in our democracies with increasing frequency, it is assumed that this is indeed the case: 'so long as I am merely speaking, and not throwing stones or bombs, I am engaged in civilised activity and civilisation itself is safe' – so runs the implicit thesis behind which lies most that is squalid and dangerous in modern, non-absolutist politics. At its best, the political activity practised by those who subscribe to the 'only sticks and stones will break my bones' thesis has the character of lurid oratory; at its worst, such activity descends to outright dishonesty, manipulation and bullying. The question is whether these unpalatable forms of political action are 'merely' morally disreputable or whether they also pose a danger to civilisation.

The answer, however unfashionable, is that such forms of

action are in fact a species of modified barbarism – and a species that is almost as threatening to the maintenance of civilised life as is the politics of the absolutist. Conforming with established constitutional practice and law is, in other words, a necessary but by no means sufficient condition for a politics that serves rather than threatens civilisation. Words have not only meanings but also effects: they change not only *what* their hearers and speakers think, but also *how* they think. If oratory is unbridled, if fact is distorted, if concepts are confused then the participants in the debate will slowly but surely begin to think of political discussion not in terms of the balanced representation of potentially equivalent principles or interests between which a contingent accommodation must be found if civilised life is to go on, but in terms akin to strife – that is, in terms of 'destroying the opposition', 'victory', 'defeat' and the like. In such a politics, the declared or covert aims of party, 'side' or faction come to dominate. In place of a recognition of the transience of each goal and the necessary contingency of each accommodation, the partisans begin to think and to make others think in terms close to those of the absolutist. 'Victory' here and now begins to mean more than the effect of the manner in which the victory was won on the ability of the society to accommodate the various principles and interests without strife in future.

In short, a constructive politics – a politics which can claim genuinely to be civilisation in the service of itself – must be one that not only identifies itself as truly political (an activity of persuasion ultimately constrained by the established practices and laws) but also one that has a sense of itself in its own history. It is the sense of history, the sense that words and manners of speaking have effects beyond their meanings, that constrains a truly constructive politics – making its practitioners conscious that in each political act, each utterance, they tilt not only the current debate but also, however slightly, the capacity of the society to continue to conduct debate itself in a manner that will permit the continuance of civilised life. To have the required sense of history is to understand that a civilisation and the framework of practice and law in which it is enshrined is an historical artefact of horrible fragility, easily destroyed, and difficult to preserve. It is to understand at the same time that each 'victory' gained by sacrificing an element of that continuity of civilised practice is actually a terrible defeat, a precedent which threatens the dissolution of the whole. To have the required sense of history is, in other words, to have a sense of the transience of the immediate not only in logical terms ('this, now, matters less than the civilisation as a whole') but also in chronological terms ('this, now, and the way in which it is achieved, matters not only or even mainly for itself but also and perhaps more importantly for the effects it will later have on the ability of society to conduct itself in a civilised fashion').

Of course, someone might object: 'this is ludicrous Puritanism – theory which has nothing to do with grass-roots politics; out there it is a jungle; your constructive politicians would not last an instant'; or, more beguilingly, 'it's all very well, and at bottom true, what you say, but the *theatre* of politics involves the low tactics you describe and these are conventions in themselves which mature politicians in a civilised society employ but place at their true worth; when they get down to serious administration or discussion behind closed doors things are different'. And to some slight – very slight – degree, these voices are right. Political debate has always been less than perfectly decorous and there is an element of acknowledged theatre. But the danger of accepting that 'anything permitted by constitutional practice and law goes', is overwhelming – and wholly ignored by the proponents of the higher cynicism. The truth is that civilisation *is* fragile and that political practice *does* have a cumulative historical effect. The way that politicians act on the political stage does affect the way in which their audiences, and ultimately they themselves, think. There is an intolerable risk that a politics conducted within the rules, but with no sense of historical effect, will slowly but surely grind away at the foundations of civilisation until at last the acknowledgement of the need to achieve by civilised means the accommodations required to continue the civilised life will give way, either directly to strife or to some form of politics of the absolute. Where the best do not act well enough, the worst may come in time to abandon all constraint.

There is also, however, an opposite danger here: that of supposing constructive politics to consist only in elegant language and courtesy. I am suggesting nothing of the sort. On the contrary, constructive politics consists in the first place in the clear-minded identification and effective advocacy of principles or interests that have been unduly neglected. The requirement to acknowledge, at least to oneself, that the goals achievable by such advocacy are logically and chronologically transient rather than ultimate, is a necessary constraint, not a sufficient description of constructive political action.

Moreover, this requirement is not satisfied by elegant evasion or courteous confusion – quite the opposite. Evasion and confusion are enemies of civilisation since they obscure the nature of the principle or interest for which the claim is being made and hence lessen rather than increase the chances of making a satisfactory contingent accommodation in any particular case. There is everything to be said for making a robust case. But, in the midst of making his robust case, the speaker needs to convey a sense that the principle or interest which he represents is clearly and honestly advocated as one amongst many rather than being overriding and ultimate.

The preconditions for constructive politics

As in other social activities – a conversation, a transaction, a trial – it is not possible for one party to engage in constructive politics unless there are counter-parties who are also engaging in the same or similar spirit. There is no point in attempting to argue constructively with absolutists, since the fundamental premiss from which argument can proceed, a shared concern with the civilisation, a recognition of the acceptance of various principles and interests, and the acceptance of the potential equivalence of each voice, are absent. Nor, on the same grounds, is there any point in trying to conduct civilised politics with outright barbarians. Nor can constructive politics persist if for whatever reasons the framework of practice and law has broken apart, to the point where there are no longer clear and accepted rules of procedure. In short, the rules of the game must be clear and the other participants must be ready to play the game in the right spirit if constructive politics is to take place.

The conduct of constructive politics is, therefore, an achievement rather than a fact of life. Civilisation requires constructive politics if it is to find civilised accommodations between the conflicting principles and interests; but what is needed is not always found. Far from it: the ability to conduct constructive politics, where it exists at all, exists tenuously – constantly under threat from all sides. Even where absolutists or outright barbarians are absent and the recognised practices and laws prevail, there may well be too few people willing to engage in politics with a sufficient sense of what is historically at stake to make clear-minded debate and resolution feasible. Where absolutism or outright barbarism are present or where (which is usually the consequence) constitutional practice and law have broken down, there may be no possibility of conducting constructive politics.

The question thus arises: what is a lover of civilisation to do when the continuance of his civilisation is threatened by the breakdown of a civilised politics capable of achieving in a civilised manner, accommodations between conflicting principles and interests? Is he to throw up his hands in horror and retire to whatever form of hermitage he can construct or find for himself, where a microcosm of the civilisation can be preserved until such time as matters improve in the big world outside? Or is he to emigrate to a place where civilised life – albeit perhaps of a somewhat different hue – continues? Certainly, both of these strategies have been adopted at various stages in history. But both are, even if individually active, socially passive: they involve as their starting point an acceptance that the society from which the émigré is fleeing is itself, at least temporarily, beyond redemption. Is there no more optimistic and socially active possibility? Must the proponent of civilisation simply cease politics when constructive politics becomes an impossibility, or is there something else he can do? These are the questions that prompt an investigation of a politics that transcends the normal constraints of civilised life in order to recreate civilised political procedure where it has broken down.

6 Transcendent Politics

The concept of transcendent politics

The term, 'transcendent politics', is an oxymoron since any form of activity which transcends or, to put it less kindly, defies the practices, and maybe even the laws in which the values of a civilisation are enshrined cannot be in the full sense 'political'. Whereas true politics is a manner of avoiding strife, transcendent politics may involve strife; whereas true politics is civilisation in the service of itself, transcendent politics involves at least a degree of barbarism.

What makes transcendent politics nevertheless importantly similar to constructive politics and hence makes it in an attenuated sense a form of politics is the shared motive. Both constructive politics and transcendent politics aim at the preservation of civilisation and both are thereby distinguished from any form of absolutism which claims ultimacity for one particular goal within a civilisation. This same feature also distinguishes transcendent politics – however illegal or violent its methods – from mere barbaric strife. For in barbaric strife people aim at particular self-interested goals whereas in transcendent politics the aim is entirely general. Transcendent politics is indeed *more general* even than normal, constructive politics. It is a second-order activity in which the proponent attempts to achieve the purely formal result of a reinstatement of civilisation instead of attempting, as in constructive politics, to promote a particular transient, substantive goal determined by a particular principle or a particular interest within the framework of a civilisation. In other words, the practices and laws which, in normal, constructive politics constitute constraints on action, and which in absolutist politics are ignored, become in transcendent politics the *object*. The aim of transcendent politics – and this is its defining characteristic – is precisely to reinstate or reinforce those practices and rules where they are under threat.

Associated with the special character of the *aim* of transcendent politics, there are special *circumstances* under which such politics can be practised. It makes no sense to engage in an activity whose sole purpose is the formal reconstitution or preservation of practices and laws if those practices and laws are in any case securely a part of the ordinary life of the community. Where the practices and laws exist, they become adverbial constraints and politics can be conducted in a normal, constructive fashion – with each actor aiming at substantive, transient goals and seeking resolution of the tensions between those goals. It is when the practice and laws of a society are obliterated or exceptionally threatened that it ceases to be rational to treat them as existing constraints. Under these circumstances, it becomes rational instead for the lover of civilisation to treat the restoration or preservation of inherited practices or laws as the sole present (though he hopes, temporary) aim of political activity.

This conception of a 'trigger' for transcendent politics is not by any means novel. For centuries, political philosophers have recognised the possibility of circumstances in which normal practices and laws can no longer be regarded as binding, due to the fact of their actual or imminent collapse. What has, however, remained unclear is the *nature* of the trigger that legitimates a change of attitude to politics and the *limits* of political action once that trigger has been principled. The principle questions in relation to transcendent politics are accordingly: what circumstances are sufficiently special to constitute a trigger, and what constraints continue to apply once transcendent politics has been triggered. Both of these questions are of the utmost theoretical and practical difficulty.

Transcendent politics as a remedy for chaos: when and how?

At a first approximation, it seems obvious that breaking the rules with the aim of restoring the effectiveness of the rules is a coherent course of action only if (1) the rules are or will with reasonable certainty very shortly be ineffective, (2) the actions taken are reasonably likely to result in the restoration of the effectiveness of the rules, and (3) the unintended consequences of the action can, with reasonable certainty, be predicted to be less harmful to the preservation of civilisation than the state of affairs which triggers the action. Each element of this proposition, however, requires elucidation.

In the first place, one has to ask: what is meant here by 'the rules'? In part, the term certainly refers to the formal laws that govern a society and that incorporate the previous resolutions of the tensions and conflicts in that society. But 'rules', here, need to be conceived more widely than simply as formal laws. Included within the concept are the rule-like practices and conventions of civilised intercourse, without which the practice of 'ordinary' constructive politics is impossible. Included also, ultimately, are the deep practices – the rule-like social constraints – that form the bedrock of civilisation: canons of taste, morality, language itself.

What is it for the 'rules', thus broadly defined, to be 'effective' or 'ineffective'? At the extremes, one has no difficulty in discerning the state of play. At the one pole lies a Hobbesian state of war – a conflict of each against all, so profound and pervasive that even the deepest rule-based social structures, even language itself, are unravelled. At the other pole lies the well-ordered society of an English village or a Swiss commune – persons well known to one another, living together, bound by the common inheritances of centuries, a social world in which any disharmony takes the form of delicately modulated nuance relying for its effectiveness on the common acceptance of a vast range of conventions and practices within which the nuances have their meaning. But for the most part, human beings live, and have always lived, in circumstances that fall at some point on the continuum between those two poles. In a big city, much that relies on commonly accepted practices and conventions persists: people speak in mutually comprehensible tongues, drive on the same side of the road, are appalled at the same crimes, expect their children to be taught roughly the same things, live in roughly similar houses, are moved by roughly the same works of art, are captivated by roughly the same adventures and admire roughly the same achievements in science and sport. And yet, in the same city, these conventions and practices are likely to be under severe threat; there are perhaps thousands of inhabitants who do not articulately share the city's language; in some parts of the city, at least, crime is rife; the assumptions about the force of law made in other neighbourhoods do not apply; disputes flare up at the least provocation about schooling, law enforcement, distribution of income, housing; taste varies widely – even to the point where some citizens live and prefer to live in what other citizens regard as wholly inappropriate ways. At what point can one say that such a city retains effective rules? At what point does one have to admit that the rules have become ineffective?

The truth is that there cannot be a clear or decisive answer. There is not a defining moment when order passes into chaos. The slide from the one to the other – this is indeed part of its insidiousness – is slow and often virtually imperceptible. The most one can say is that there are certain criteria by which the effectiveness of 'normal rules' can be judged. These include: the ability of the citizens, by and large, to communicate effectively with one another; the common assumption of similar basic moral precepts which are at the same time enshrined in law (an injunction, for example, against murder or theft); the usual, if not invariable, enforcement of law by recognised and effective procedures; the existence of a civil power capable, at the ultimate, of quelling riot or violence; the ability of each citizen to go about his or her daily business largely unimpeded by violent disruption. When a large number of these criteria are to a significant degree unfulfilled, the situation can fairly be characterised as one in which the 'rules' have become ineffective. But the judgement will always remain: how many criteria have to apply, and to what degree, before the rules can truly be said to be ineffective?

Nor is this the only judgement required in the justification of a transcendent political action. Very frequently, the justification will be not that the rules *are* ineffective, but that they will shortly be so. In such a case, one has to ask what it is to be 'reasonably certain' of their coming ineffectiveness. And one has also to ask what is the test of 'reasonable likelihood' that the action in question will result in the restoration of the effectiveness of the rules. One point, here, is clear – the test of 'reasonable certainty' is, and ought to be, tougher than the test of 'reasonable likelihood'. If normal, civilised life is almost certainly about to break down, it is reasonable to take actions outside the normal rules in an effort to restore normal life, even if the degree of certainty attaching to the effectiveness of the remedy is less great than the degree of certainty with which the disease is diagnosed. As the medical analogy indicates, one ought not to take drastic action except when one can be *very* confident that its absence will be catastrophic; but, when one is so confident, the drastic action may be justified even where one cannot be confident of its success.

The inevitably difficult questions of judgement involved in the diagnosis of disorder and in the prediction of the effects of a drastic remedy are not by any means the end of the matter. There is also the horribly difficult judgement whether the remedy, even if in its own terms likely to be effective, may have side-effects so deleterious to civilisation as to render it worse than useless. Here, again, there can be no clear answers. One can, at best, list relevant criteria which include: the degree and extent of suffering caused by the remedy; the extent to which this suffering may give rise to a lasting resentment that will threaten instability hereafter; the extent to which the action *does* breach the rules that it sets out to restore; the duration of the disruption of the rules by the action – i.e. the time elapsing or likely to elapse before the rules are restored; and the precedent set by the action – its impact upon the acceptance, hereafter, of the rules that it consciously breaks today. Whilst it is well nigh impossible to be sure in advance when these criteria are sufficiently met, there are clear historical cases where – in retrospect – the side-effects were (or were not) sufficiently ghastly to make the transcendent action counter-productive. General Monk and the restoration of Charles II lie on the favourable side of the line; the Greek colonels and the removal of democracy, on the unfavourable side.

Transcendent politics, tyranny and revolution

To any student of history, the identification of the breakdown or ineffectiveness of 'the rules' as a prime trigger for exceptional political action will seem strange. The imposition by force of order on chaos – though practised by kings since time out of mind, understood by Hobbes and often enough, also, experienced in the late 20th century – has not been, in the history of political thought, the predominant example of exceptional political activity, or the form of such activity that has most preoccupied the theorists. It is, rather, revolution against tyranny that has played these roles in our intellectual history. Traditionally, the question has been, not 'under what circumstances should strong action be taken to restore order?', but instead, 'under what circumstances can revolution be justified in the face of tyranny?' And to this question, also, the theory of transcendent politics has an answer.

In the first place, the theory readily provides a definition of the moment when any popular government crosses the line into tyranny. The moment – often very difficult to identify in practice – comes when the tyrant or the tyrannical gang cease to practise an 'ordinary' practical politics and fail to provide any opportunity for others to restore the practice of such politics except through revolution. It is the moment, in short, when politics ceases to be, even potentially, civilisation in the service of itself. The signs of this line having been crossed are: a disregard by the tyrant of established law, practice and convention; a disregard of principles other than those with which the tyrant is concerned and/or of interests other than those of the tyrant himself; and, critically, a regime within which there is no practical means other than revolution by which these disregards can be remedied. The politics of a tyranny is solipsistic – politics in the service of itself, rather than politics in the service of civilisation.

Beyond this definition of the character of tyranny, the theory of transcendent politics also provides an account of the *form* of conduct permissible in revolutionary conditions (the 'how') and of the 'trigger' conditions (the 'when') which make revolutionary action legitimate.

So far as the 'when' is concerned, two principles can be deduced from the fundamental relationship between politics and civilisation: (1) revolutionary activity is legitimate only when the solipsistic disregards and the prevention of ordinary means of remedy that are the hallmarks of tyranny are so severe as to render it incoherent or irrational to attempt, within the constraints of the tyrannical regime's law and practice, to represent particular principles other than those sponsored by the tyrant or any interests other than those of the tyrant himself; and (2) even where the first condition is fulfilled, revolutionary activity (just like transcendent activity to restore order in circumstances of chaos) is legitimate only when the action, taking its direct and indirect consequences together, is sufficiently likely to promote rather than to diminish the chances of restoring the civilised conduct of politics. These two conditions – lack of a coherent alternative and a high chance of success even after the indirect consequences are taken into account – together constitute the very demanding criteria which are each a necessary, and are together a sufficient basis for revolutionary action.

So far as the 'how' is concerned, the principles are precisely in line with the criteria for the 'when': revolution against tyranny, as an example of transcendent politics, must be conducted in such a fashion as to minimise the short- and long-term damage done to the fabric of the civilisation.

As in the case of transcendent activity to reimpose order on chaos, it is vastly easier to set these general principles than to tell in practice whether a particular revolution obeys the principles. One can in the light of subsequent developments assert that the Glorious Revolution was properly conducted in a sense that the Russian revolution was not – not least because the Russian revolution, unlike the Glorious Revolution, was an example of absolutism rather than transcendent political activity, (activity with a transient aim represented as an absolute rather than activity with a pure aim of changing the framework of political action). But it is difficult, if not impossible, to judge, even at our current historical remove, whether either or both of these events qualified as legitimate in terms of the existence of a 'trigger' for transcendent action. There is no escaping from this difficulty: those fomenting revolution who are also lovers of civilisation will perennially find the experience nightmarish and it is *right* that they should find it so: to disturb the established order and to do so in the belief that one will establish an order more conducive to the conduct of a civilised, political politics is an act that should trouble any conscience attuned to the magnitude of the evils potentially attending the act. Anybody fitted to be a transcendent revolutionary will be acutely worried by being one.

The question, 'when?' applied to transcendent politics, is thus a question that has to be answered in many parts and can never be answered by a lover of civilisation with absolute assurance. It is, however, possible to be closer to absolute assurance in answer to the question, 'how?' because the constraints on transcendent politics can be derived logically from its character. To be, however tenuously, a political act as opposed to a form of absolutism posing as transcendent, any action taken in contravention of the rules must have as its aim (and as its reasonably likely result) restoration of those rules. Hence, the action cannot be of a form which, either directly or indirectly, through precedent or resentment, threatens either the early restoration or the long-term stability of the normal practices and conventions of the civilised society. In short, the action must be swift, decisive, and manifestly out of the ordinary, and it must be, and be seen to be, conducted with as little infringement of the residually present (even if presently ineffective) practices and conventions as possible. These conditions are, in fact, significantly restrictive and hence significantly descriptive. Whilst one cannot say, abstracted from particular circumstances, how swift is 'swift', how decisive is 'decisive', how extraordinary is 'extraordinary' or how little infringement is possible, one can with relative ease in practice distinguish between, for example, Mao's cultural revolution and the American Revolution. The cultural revolution – in any case motivated by egalitarian absolutism of the most determined kind – was as prolonged, as tortuous, as far a way of life and as disruptive of pre-existing practices as it was able to be; Washington's handling of the American Revolution, by contrast, as well as being motivated by a desire to re-establish deeply set practices and conventions of civility rather than by any transient aim, was as fast, as conclusive, as avowedly exceptional and as observant of the pre-existing conventions as its fomenters knew how to make it. Whether, in practice, the colonists' action was justified by any sufficient ineffectiveness of 'the rules' at the time it took place, is a matter for continuing and probably endless controversy and speculation: but it was at least in stark contrast to the actions of the cultural revolution, and conducted in a *manner* suitable to transcendent politics.

Transcendent politics, nationhood and international relations

The case of the American Revolution (unlike a merely domestic revolution) raises a range of questions beyond the 'how' and 'when' of revolutionary action within a single society – questions of a global nature and of the greatest possible importance and difficulty. What, if anything, justifies the assertion of nationhood or statehood in contravention of pre-existing practices? And, once extant, how are nations or states to relate to one another? It is in the context of these questions that the concept of transcendent politics has its most widespread application. The idea of a nation or of a 'people' is, notoriously amongst political theorists, fuzzy. In part racial, in part cultural, the term 'nation' denotes no more than a set of inheritances sufficiently strong to make many, if not all, of the inheritors regard themselves as sufficiently similar to one another and different to others to call themselves part of one nation. In short, its fuzziness derives from the fact that, instead of being a legal or political form, it consists of a civilisation with a marked degree of self-consciousness. Of course, any such self-conscious civilisation will be kaleidoscopically related not only to its own past but also to overlapping and contiguous civilisations: the degree of self-consciousness may or may not be matched by an equivalently clear, objective distinction between the nation itself and the civilisations with which it is kaleidoscopically related. Nevertheless, when it comes to civilisation, the consciousness of difference *is* difference – and there can thus be no denying that a nation conscious of its own identity constitutes in the fullest sense of the term a distinct civilisation.

Now the question arises: is there any reason why a nation, so conceived, need be also a state? Taken one way, the answer to this question is manifestly: no. The Scots may conceive themselves as a nation without necessarily being a state; the Germans in times past may have conceived of themselves as being a nation whilst being many states. Statehood is a matter of law, nationhood is a matter of self-awareness – the two may diverge. But to say that they *may* diverge is *not* to say that there is no intrinsic connection between them. On the contrary, there *is* such a connection. The state, as a legal entity, enshrines in its formalities some of the deepest practices of its members, the resolution of tensions that have arisen between them. Hence, the state will have, inevitably, a cultural character: it will be a state belonging to *this* civilisation rather than to some other. It is, therefore, entirely understandable, even if not necessary or inevitable, that a people who conceive of themselves as a nation, a distinct civilisation, should wish to see the character of that civilisation enshrined in and protected by a state-of-their-own.

It is a point of the utmost importance that the effort of a nation to create for itself a state is not an absolutist act. There is no transient, substantive aim being raised to the level of the absolute. The aim is 'merely' to establish a framework within which the formal legal structure will reflect the particularities of the civilisation in question – the particularities that render, for example, French civilisation and German civilisation recognisably different subsets of European civilisation. At the same time, however, this is not a 'normal' aim of constructive politics. It is not a case of seeking a transient aim whilst observing the pre-existing practice. It is, rather, an archetypal example of transcendent politics – an effort to make effective a set of values which (in this case for want of a state) have not previously been in effect.

Once the transcendent character of the effort on the part of a nation to create a state-of-its-own is understood, the constraints on such efforts become more nearly apparent in the light of the fundamental thesis that the ultimate purpose of politics is the preservation of civilisation. As with any form of transcendent politics, the constraints must clearly consist of the requirement that the actions, if not sanctioned by an existing framework (e.g. through an agreed act of decolonisation) should not be undertaken except when (1) it is at least reasonably certain that the act is in its own terms necessary – i.e. that the rules-in-concept will not otherwise become peaceably effective, (2) it is at least reasonably likely that the action will result in such effectiveness of the rules-in-concept, and (3) there is reasonable certainty that the act will not, from the point of view of the sustenance of the civilisation, be counter-productive – due in part to the fact that the action, when taken, is as swift, decisive, extra-ordinary and non-disruptive of the rules-in-concept as may be. Subject to the observance of these constraints, there cannot be any ultimate objection on the part of the lover of civilisation to the attempt by a nation to foster its own survival by enshrining itself in a state-of-its-own.

The next question is how states, once formed, should behave in relation to one another: and it is in answer to this question that the full power of the concept of transcendent politics in the international sphere reveals itself. The theory of international relations (which, with the notable exceptions of Kant and passingly Aristotle, has not attracted much attention from the most significant philosophers) has been dominated by more or less subtle variations of three respectable alternative theses. These can be described, respectively, as: nationalism, internationalism and imperialism. 'Nationalism', here, is shorthand for what are, in fact, several connected theses: the nationalist believes in the right of each people (and hence, at least, of each state) to self- determination; he argues that authority and law are meaningful terms only in the context of one another, and in the context of a state endowed with rules and a sovereign capable of enforcing these rules according to accepted procedures. From these two propositions – the right of self-determination allied to the meaninglessness of law outside the context of a state – the nationalist derives the view that (1) all external acts of the state are bound to be governed by the interest of that state rather than by any form of international right, (2) no state, however, has reason to impose upon another, and (3) international relations, therefore, have the character of, at best, an unregulated market of rational but self-interested agents striking bargains with one another or, at worst, (and in the absence of mutually acceptable bargains) a war of each against all. Internationalism, by contrast, consists of the thesis that human society stretches beyond the boundaries of the state, that it is in consequence entirely possible to construct, discuss and enforce international law, and that it is ultimately desirable to construct a single international authority for the human race as a guarantee of everlasting peace. The imperialist sits between the nationalist and the internationalist – agreeing with the nationalist that law can be conceived only within the context of the state but believing (like the internationalist) that ways of life appropriate to the entire human race can be deduced by the enlightened; and from these premisses, the imperialist derives the view that it is the solemn duty of the enlightened state to impose its law upon the benighted people whose intellects have failed to discern the true path.

Alongside each of these three, respectable theses, there is a 'bad version' of the thesis, employed by robber barons and megalomaniacs. In these 'bad' versions, nationalism is used to justify unrestricted bellicosity; internationalism is used to justify universal interference; and imperialism is used to justify global colonisation – in short, the three theses are made for all practical purposes to collapse into the single thesis that might is right. But there is no need to dwell on the 'bad' versions of the theses; the existence of robber barons (though hugely important in practice) is of no theoretical interest to the lover of civilisation since the views of such thugs certainly will not provide a guiding light for the well-intentioned. The true intellectual problem is not that the two versions exist; it is that even the respectable versions of the three theses are all sadly lacking. Nationalism, like other forms of reductionism, suffers from the grave defect of being philosophically daring rather than truthful: the nationalist seeks to 'sweep away all the clap-trap about international law and principles of human society', and in so doing ends by making the brave but cognitively dissonant assertion that there is absolutely nothing that can guide the conduct of states in the absence of mutually acceptable bargains, no abiding principles of how one state should treat the citizens of another, nothing in principle wrong with unconstrained warfare under circumstances of aggression, no limits to the horrors that can legitimately be perpetrated in the name of the state despite the fact that such things within the state itself would be counted as violent crimes. The internationalist, with his richer ontology, rescues himself from such dry cynicism. But in so doing, he fails to acknowledge first, the evident difference between law in the context of a state and so-called 'international law', and second, the very strong attachment of each nation to its own highly distinct and idiosyncratic mode of self-government. The imperialist, meanwhile, is left in the intolerable position of defending – typically without more than prejudice at root – his own methods as intrinsically superior and himself as an intrinsically superior governor not merely for his own nation, but for others, thereby ignoring the force of a nationalist's attachment to self-determination.

These deficiencies of nationalism, internationalism and imperialism can be remedied by applying to the sphere of international relations both the general thesis that politics ought to be civilisation in the service of itself and, in particular, the principles of transcendent politics which derive from that general thesis. The application, both of the general thesis and of its transcendent derivative to the field of international relations is, in fact, straightforward. If one begins with the proposition that the purpose of politics in general is the preservation and promotion of civilisation it follows (1) that there is some value to be attributed to the preservation of civilisation *as such* – that is, to the preservation and promotion of each and every civilisation; (2) that actions tending to the elimination or destruction of any civilisation are *ipso facto* an evil (albeit, in some cases, a necessary evil); (3) that any action tending to the diminution or destruction of any civilisation can only conceivably be justified by its tendency to produce disproportionate enhancement of another civilisation, and (4) that, to the extent that a civilisation is embodied in a state (i.e. to the extent that a state represents not the triumph of an abstract absolutism but rather a web of resolutions of the tensions inherent in that civilisation) an attack on a state represents an attempt to diminish or destroy at least one instantiation of that civilisation and is thus *ipso facto* an evil which can be justified only, if at all, by an overwhelming enhancement of another civilisation.

Beyond these general principles, particularities of the permissible can be deduced from the observation that the field of international affairs is *par excellence* a field of transcendent politics. In the case of international affairs, the cause of the requirement for transcendence is not merely the temporary ineffectiveness of the rules which is (very rarely) witnessed within a state; the cause of the need for transcendence in this context is, rather, the fact that accepted and effectively enforced 'rules' are pervasively and perennially *absent*. The field of international relations is a field in which, precisely, there is no over-riding authority capable of effectively enforcing any set of rules: were there such an authority it would constitute a state and the field of play would become domestic rather than international. For so long as the international exists as a phenomenon, it is a field of endeavour in which no rules are effectively enforced – and hence a field of endeavour in which 'ordinary constructive' politics are impossible.

Accordingly, the only non-absolutist principles that can apply to international affairs– if any principles at all attractive to the lover of civilisation are to apply – are those of transcendent politics and, in particular, the principles of transcendent politics that apply under circumstances in which transcendent action is required to restore rules which have become ineffective – circumstances of anarchy.

The first precondition of transcendent politics is, of course, fulfilled in an international setting to a far greater extent than could ever be the case in a state: the rules, so far as these are international in character, are by hypothesis and for sure ineffective – they simply do not exist as a set of enforceable constraints. The second precondition is, however, far more contentious. Under what circumstances could a lover of civilisation reasonably maintain that an action in international relations will lead to the 'restoration' of 'the rules' in a particular locality? The answer to this question takes us to the depths of international affairs.

We have to ask, first, in what sense can an international situation pose a threat to the continuity of 'the rules' of a particular locality and hence of the civilisation of that locality? Broadly, potential causes of such disruption are: invasion by another state of one's own; actions by another state calculated to cause chaos in one's own state; and internal chaos in another state. The first two of these are situations recognisable to a nationalist; the third (far more difficult) is recognisable to the benevolent imperialist. In the first two cases, the civilisation under threat is one's own. The threat is to the preservation of 'the rules' of one's own state, and hence to the ability of that state to continue to embody and protect the practices and conventions which are constitutive of one's own civilisation. The response is to resist invasion or to prevent destabilisation – if necessary, by force. As with transcendent politics within a state, such actions (likely as they are to damage the offending state and hence the civilisation which it embodies) are to be justified only if they are reasonably likely to succeed and only if it is, in addition, reasonably certain that they will not have unintended consequences more damaging than the failure to act. The notion of 'damaging' is, of course, contentious: is one to take into account damage to one's own civilisation or damage to that of the offending state, or, if (as the lover of civilisation is bound to hold) of both, then how balanced against one another? The question of balance, as in the case of transcendent politics within the context of a single state, is difficult and necessarily uncertain in the outcome. The most that can be said in the abstract is that the only position from which such questions can rationally be answered for the lover of civilisation is from behind a Rawlsian veil of ignorance. One has to ask: 'if I do not know which civilisation or state I would be a member of, what actions would I sponsor?' This almost impossibly difficult question does no more than to attempt to put the enquirer in a suitably Olympian position. The horribly intractable problem of uncertainty remains – and resists any theoretical advance. Only in practice, and then only by guesswork, do particular answers emerge in particular circumstances.

In many respects, matters are simpler when the offending state – the invading or destabilising state – is *not* itself an embodiment of a civilisation but is, rather, so thoroughly in the hands of the barbarians or absolutists that it has become a threat to the survival of its own civilisation. Frequently enough, where there is invasion or destabilisation, this will indeed be the case. And where it is the case, resistance by force (even if carried to the extent of reciprocal invasion or destabilisation) is relatively uncontroversial to a lover of civil-

THE PURPOSE OF POLITICS

isation, since the net benefit to civilisation, considered from behind a veil of ignorance, is easier to determine. The Second World War is a case in point.

Matters become difficult – hideously difficult – again when it comes to transcendent actions by one state aimed not at self-preservation but at restoring the effectiveness of the rules within another state. In theory, the case for action is straightforward and of exactly the same character as in the situation of self-defence. Indeed, from behind the veil of ignorance, there is no difference between the two cases: the problem is, rather, one of moral hazard. How is one to distinguish in practice between transcendent action genuinely aimed solely at the restoration of 'the rules' – i.e. the practices and conventions in which the civilisation of that nation is enshrined – from an imperialist act, arising from the desire to impose one's own rules, alien as they are, on the nation upon whom they are being imposed? No advance can be made in such situations by a resort to the language of internationalism (the 'international community', 'international law') since this, like the imperialist's position, ignores rather than reinforces the claims of the indigenous civilisation and its own practices and conventions. Here theory can guide no further: one is in the realm of practical judgements and self-awareness. The most that can be said at the level of theory is that an act of interference may be justified in the exceptional circumstances where – in the terms set for itself by another civilisation – 'the rules' peculiar to the society that instantiates that civilisation have with reasonable certainty broken down, where there is a reasonable likelihood that intervention will make those rules (and not some others imported from without) again effective, and where it is reasonably certain that the act will not, in terms of that civilisation, be ultimately counter-productive. An actor, aware of the moral hazard in such a case (the danger that the intervention is in fact justified only on the false basis of imperialism or internationalism) should certainly apply these normal standards of transcendent action particularly harshly in such a case: and even then with a real risk of mistake.

In sum, the theory of transcendent political action cannot make simplicity where there is difficulty; what it can do, is to provide a conceptual framework more subtle and more adequate than nationalism, internationalism or imperialism for thinking about international relations. For those lovers of civilisation who adopt that framework, there remain inevitably doubts and reservations. But there is at least a sense of direction and restraint. International relations are to be guided by the desire: (1) to preserve and enhance civilisations everywhere; to defend one's own civilisation certainly – but to favour one's own only to the extent and in ways that one would choose if one were considering the matter behind a veil of ignorance about one's own location; (2) to act with an ever-present sense of the need to concern oneself both with the integrity of other civilisations and with the likely effects (positive and negative) of one's actions upon such other civilisations as well as upon one's own; (3) to recognise the claim of a nation, a civilisation aware of itself, to have a state-of-its-own, but to expect it to observe the same civilising constraints upon its own efforts at self-realisation; and (4) to be prepared to intervene when 'the rules' of another state have become ineffective – but only where the harshest tests have been passed to minimise the moral hazard of an intervention unconsciously or semi-consciously based on internationalism or imperialism. If the actions of one state towards another were governed solely by these constraints, the world would not, of course, be a perfect place. It would still be marred by many mistakes of practical judgement. But it would be, from the point of view of a lover of civilisation, a much better place.

III Arguments and Conclusions

7 Can One Argue for a View of Politics?

The status of the thesis

The purpose of the preceding chapters has been to illustrate the nature of civilisation and the role that politics, both constructive and transcendent, can play in its preservation, as well as the way in which the disturbed 'visionary' politics of the absolutists can militate against civilisation. Such illustrations do not, however, in themselves establish the importance of the thesis that the ultimate aim of politics is the promotion and preservation of civilisation. This thesis, accompanied by the illustrations, may of course be immediately attractive to any lover of civilisation; but attractiveness is not the same thing as significance, and the question therefore remains: does the thesis have any explanatory power?

There are at least five respects in which the thesis does seem to have explanatory power:

- it explains why so many false assertions can have been made in the past explicitly or implicitly about the ultimate aim of politics;
- it explains the relationship between politics and ethics;
- it elucidates how one state should behave vis-à-vis others;
- it provides a framework within which one can begin to

address the challenge of the 'underclass'; and
- it explains the persistence of the particularly poignant and fundamental tensions between the principle of freedom and the principle of community.

Truth everywhere

In a slight adaptation of Wittgenstein's famous example of the duck-rabbit, two spectators, observing the same picture from two vantage points, conclude that what they are seeing is in the first case a duck and in the second case a rabbit; the discrepancy between their views leads two commentators to different conclusions. The first commentator concludes that both of the observers are mistaken since the picture is neither of a duck or a rabbit but of both. The second commentator concludes that at least one of the observers is mistaken since the picture may be either of a duck or of a rabbit but cannot be simultaneously a picture of both. Which of the commentators is right?

The answer, of course, is that the commentators are both wrong because the observers are both – to a degree – right. True, the picture is not simply of a duck or simply of a rabbit; seen from a certain angle it *looks* like a picture of a duck, and seen from another angle it *looks* like a picture of a rabbit. In other words, each of the observers is missing the nature of the whole and overstating the importance of a particular appearance, but each is nevertheless 'onto' something.

This example stands for a world of similar incidents and conditions – in which observers, regarding objects and situations from different perspectives, argue vehemently in favour of what *appear* to be conflicting descriptions but are *actually* partial appearances of a whole whose complex nature is hidden from all of the participants. And this pattern of partial perception is exactly what mars the history of thought about the ultimate purpose of politics.

The various theses examined in Chapter 1 – the theses that politics has as its ultimate goal freedom, or equality, or justice, or virtue, or beauty, or truth, or prosperity, or power – are all, if conceived as complete descriptions, false for the reasons identified in that chapter. Unfettered freedom is worthless or worse. Equality, to the extent that it can be coherently described as an ultimate aim would – if so pursued – fail entirely to recognise the claims of justice and liberty. Justice as an ultimate aim neglects the claim of freedom, and virtue equally neglects the claim of justice. Beauty and truth – if advanced as full descriptions of the ultimate aim – give no due weight to the entire realm of the moral; and prosperity and power are properly to be conceived as instrumental rather than absolute items – means not ends. Inspecting these various failed attempts to offer a description of the ultimate aim of politics, one might be tempted, like the first commentator in the duck-rabbit story, to conclude that all of the theoreticians are simply wrong: but (like that commentator) in making such a claim, one would be missing at least as much as all of the theorists themselves. For whilst it is true that freedom, equality, justice, virtue, beauty, truth, prosperity and power are each woefully incomplete descriptions of what politics ought to be aiming at, they are all also partially correct descriptions; the proponents of each are 'onto' something. The first advantage of the thesis of this book (that the preservation of civilisation is the true ultimate aim of politics) is that it can explain both what the various observers are 'onto' and what they are missing. If the thesis is correct, then each of the proffered ultimates with the exception of power is a basic principle within civilisation; and power is the means by which (or, more exactly, is the measure of the extent to which) within the political arrangements of civilised society, the proponents of a given principle are able in particular, concrete circumstances to achieve a favourable resolution. That freedom, equality, justice, virtue, beauty, truth and prosperity *are* all or may all be principles recognised within the civilisation is a proposition so evident as almost to require no further elaboration. It is, however, worth emphasising that – in drawing our attention to these values – the major thinkers in the history of western political thought have elaborated not merely *possible* principles but the most significant and continuous and pervasive principles of Western civilisation. It is, in short, almost a defining characteristic at least of Western civilisation, taken in the broadest sense, that these values are – each and all – celebrated.

To an inheritor of Western civilisation, a society in which freedom is not valued appears lacking in the sense that it fails to recognise both the intrinsic significance of self-determination and the vast potential of human creativity. The fundamental nature of the Western attachment to freedom is indicated by the oddity of the question 'why does it matter?' We have no adequate answer because the importance of self-determination and of the potential for creativity seems to us obvious: they are part of the intellectual and emotional bedrock of our lives. To question them is to question whether human life is as we conceive it. We want to be free because we want to be free. The same applies – *mutatis mutan-dis* – to each of the other apparent 'ultimate' aims of politics: equality, justice, virtue, beauty, truth and prosperity. For us, as inheritors of Western civilisation, each of these is to be justified not in terms of some further goal but as an end in itself. We wish to avoid undue disparities, to see fair treatment for all, to promote moral virtue, to create and preserve beauty, to discover truth and to lead a life of prosperous ease… because we wish these things. So far as we are concerned (and it is exactly the phrase we would naturally use), a society is less civilised if its inhabitants are unfree, hugely disparate in material circumstances and education, unjustly governed, lacking in moral standards, surrounded by ugliness, ignorant of the truth and widely impoverished. But at the same time, and for the same reason, no one of these is in truth *the* ultimate value of our civilisation, since no one of these has general or absolute priority over the others. Western civilisation, in other words, implies the ultimately irresolvable tension between *each* of these values. Theoreticians are all 'onto' something when they identify the absolute validity of their respective favourites. But they are missing the manifold of which the values are all constituent parts – the manifold, or complex of inter-locking manifolds, which constitutes Western civilisation. In short, the theoreticians have correctly identified a range of ultimate values, but have missed the nature of the civilisation as the complex within which all of these values have their place and which, taken as a whole, has a worth superior to the pursuit *ad ultimum* of any single constituent value. It is a problem not of seeing what is not there but of not seeing all that is there. In describing the problem thus, the thesis of this book gives an account of how immensely clever people thinking hard over the centuries can have disagreed so vehemently with one another – the plausibility of which account derives from the fact that the dispute can be seen to follow the duck-rabbit pattern so common in other parts of the history of ideas.

The paradox of morality in politics

The second claim to be made for the thesis that the ultimate purpose of politics is the preservation of civilisation, is that this thesis can provide a coherent picture of the subtle and problematic relationship between political action and moral action.

Are political actions *ipso facto* to be classified as moral actions? If so, the people who are responsible for them will typically be responsible for a large number of either morally good or morally bad acts. Now, a person who is responsible for a bad act (even a voluntarily bad act) need not be a bad person: he may have made an error of judgement or have fallen temporarily prey to temptation. But there is at least a *prima facie* case for supposing that a person who constantly performs voluntary acts that are bad is a bad person; so, if political acts are *ipso facto* moral acts, a government which constantly performed badly would *prima facie* be composed of bad people – and all those citizens who supported, aided or implemented the actions of such a government would be *prima facie* bad people. This naïve view of the moral character of political action, if true, would lead both to the extremities of pessimism about the human condition and the destruction of any significant argument for democracy. If it were really the case that constantly bad political decision-making implied moral evil on the part of those making, supporting or implementing such decisions, we would be forced to conclude both that we are surrounded by a great deal of such evil and that a system in which decisions are ratified by a majority – rather than by good people alone – is itself evil and corrupt: there is, after all, no more reason to suppose that moral decisions are to be arrived at by majority voting than that matters of truth and falsity should be so decided. Indeed, it is just such a view, and just such a chain of argument, that led Plato to the conclusion that – so far from democracy – the only appropriate regime for a society is one in which all power is exercised by those few individuals who possess true moral wisdom; and, in a diluted form, this same reasoning led Aristotle to the same conclusion. If political action *is* moral action, then the problem of politics becomes the identification of the morally good people, and the correct politics becomes one in which all power is handed to those people.

Those of us who advocate democratic decision-making are thus bound either to resort to the feeble and implausible claim that democracy is the best system for identifying moral virtue in potential rulers; or to abandon our deeply held attachment to democracy in favour of some more rational basis for selecting a virtuous government; or to reject the view that political action *is* moral action. The third of these possibilities – the rejection of any naïve identification of political action as moral action – seems by far the preferable choice, not least because it accords with the view that most decent people take and have traditionally taken of political opponents. It has been customary, and remains customary in civilised societies, to distinguish between disagreement at a political level and disapproval at the moral level. One *wants* to be able to make such a distinction because it frequently seems *true* that a political opponent is nevertheless morally upright: and it seems true also, alas, that some political allies are less than morally upright.

An apparently easy way to preserve the distinction between morality and politics is to adopt the view that the two have nothing whatsoever to do with one another – that politics is a wholly amoral, prudential affair, in which decisions are to be classed either as useful or as counter-productive, without any suggestion of a moral content. On this view, democratic decision-making becomes a rational means of expressing prudential preferences and of resolving disputes between differing prudential preferences; and the politicians and bureaucrats who propose and implement such preferences may be (morally speaking) good, bad or indifferent people, regardless of the particular prudential decisions that they are proposing or implementing. But this view is at least as implausible as its counterpart-doctrine that political action *is* moral action. The complete separation of political action from moral character fails because it suggests that the worst we can say about Hitler, Stalin and Mao is that, whatever their personal moral standing may have been, their political acts were 'counter-productive'; whereas, in fact, we want to be able to say what seems abundantly true – that *their* political actions (even if not all misplaced political actions) were *evil*. And the attempt to de-link politics wholly from morality faces the same problem in the opposite direction: it suggests that the best we can say about Wilberforce's campaign to abolish slavery was that it was useful. This is simply not enough – Wilberforce was *right, morally* right.

So we have an apparent paradox. On the one side, it seems clear that political action is not to be equated naively with moral action. On the other side, it seems clear that political action is not to be distinguished wholly from moral action. One ostensibly comforting way of resolving this paradox would be to argue that, whilst most acts of government (and most political actions) are merely prudent or imprudent, certain extreme acts – or acts in certain extreme circumstances – may be morally good or bad. At first hearing, this distinction of the normal from the extreme has the ring of plausibility. But upon further examination the distinction proves to offer very little help, if any. In the first place, it simply moves the problem back a step – leaving us searching for a definition of the dividing-line which sufficiently differentiates extreme actions and circumstances from the normal to explain the huge leap from the world of merely prudential decision to the world of moral decision. And, relatedly, it leaves us puzzling about why, if extreme political acts (such as Auschwitz or the freeing of the slaves) can be – as they undoubtedly can be – *very* evil or *very* good, other and less extreme acts are not capable of being *quite* evil or *quite* good instead of being merely counter-productive or useful.

Another apparently comfortable resolution of the apparent paradox lies in the assertion that, whereas a large *range* of political acts may be morally *neutral* (and hence fall to be judged only in terms of their usefulness or counter-productivity) other kinds of act falling outside the neutral range have moral implications and are therefore either good or evil. But this comfort, too, is denied us upon further inspection – because it leaves us with precious little clue to the method of distinguishing acts that are in the supposed neutral range from those outside that range. Almost every political action appears to have, upon close examination, *some* moral implication (some effect upon the moral lives of those whom it affects); so moral neutrality cannot be equated, here, with lack of moral effect. Moreover, the motives of a political actor will almost always have a moral quality (a politician acts out of higher or lower motive, nobility of purpose or low cunning), so that political acts will typically have both moral motives and moral effects: in what, then, does any supposed moral neutrality lie?

Finally, it might be thought that the paradox is to be resolved by reference to the possibility of *error*. One might argue, for instance, that certain political actions which fall away from usefulness do so only to the extent of being prudential mistakes, whereas other represent so great a departure from the appropriate pattern as to be beyond the limits of prudential error, and hence fall into the category of the evil. But this avenue, too, looks less and less promising as one travels down it. In ordinary life (outside politics), we do not hold that an intentional act consciously taken by its perpetrator moves from being the subject of prudential judgement to being the subject of moral judgement depending upon the *extent* of the error contained in it. If the *character* of the error is moral (e.g. if it involves selfishness or vainglory) then the act is (albeit in many cases only slightly) immoral. Whereas, if the character of the error is prudential (e.g. if it involves honestly and non-negligently mistaking friends for enemies in wartime) then we think of the act as morally neutral, notwithstanding the fact that the effects may be horrendous. And if, in ordinary life, we class error (regardless of its size) as in this way either prudential or moral, why should we adopt a different view in the field of political action? What is more, any such attempt at resolution of the paradox in terms of error leaves us with a yawning gap when it comes to virtuous political acts. How is one, for example, to explain the moral rectitude of the freeing of the slaves in terms of the absence of prudential error? The whole point is that the act had a justification which went beyond the field of the prudential and was hence not to be thought of as useful, but as *right*. Here, prudence or counter-productivity (and hence also the relation of the act to prudential error) is an irrelevance.

The apparent paradox that political action appears both to have moral connotations and yet not to be *ipso facto* moral in character is, then, a deep problem rather than a superficial difficulty to be lightly tossed aside. It is, therefore, an indication of the explanatory power of the thesis of this book – the thesis that the prime aim of politics is the preservation of civilisation – that it can comprehensively and coherently resolve the paradox. The resolution begins with the observation that if the prime aim of politics is the preservation of civilisation, then the underlying purpose of politics is moral – since the morality of a society (as described in Chapter 2) is an integral part of the civilisation of that society, and whatever aims to preserve or tends to preserve that civilisation *ipso facto* aims to preserve or tends to preserve the morality inherent in it. This is what explains the intrinsically moral connotations of political action. It is also what explains the fact that certain forms of political action can be morally evil: namely, the politics of the absolute and the politics of unrestrained self-interest – both of which are types of barbarism intrinsically hostile to (and destructive of) civilisation, and both of which, therefore, tend to undermine the basis for morality in a society where they are practised. By disregarding, instead of reinforcing, the order of normal peaceful transactions between the citizenry and the conditions (*inter alia*, the moral conditions) that, within the civilisation, govern such transactions, these forms of political action constitute a direct attack upon the morality of the society and are hence, in the full sense, evil. To put this another way, the morality practised within a civilisation will demand of its members (as a necessary precondition for the survival of that civilisation) that they respect the various principles within that civilisation. Political actions springing either out of an absolute adherence to a particular principle or out of unrestrained self-interest and which as a consequence ride roughshod over the consideration of other principles or persons, contradict that fundamental moral obligation. For example, the adherents of egalitarian absolutism ride roughshod over the principle of truth (as in the propaganda and show trials of totalitarian communist states) and, in so doing, incite the citizenry to disregard the respect for truth that constitutes an important moral obligation within our civilisation. Such destructive, absolutist or unrestrainedly self-interested political acts convict those who engage in them of moral evil on a large or small scale.

At the same time, however, the thesis that the prime aim

of politics is the preservation of civilisation can explain why it is possible and coherent for decent people to disagree about political actions, and to take opposing practical political steps without accusing or suspecting one another of moral turpitude. Truly *political* politics – the form of politics conducted by those who, whilst they may be forwarding the claim of a particular principle, are not acting either out of unconstrained self-interest or in disregard of the other principles within the society – is in itself a moral *good*: it tends (as it aims) towards the preservation of the civilisation within which it takes place and thus (albeit indirectly) tends also towards the preservation of the morality of that civilisation. Those advocating the cause of a particular principle at a given moment in the history of civilisation will, nevertheless, typically disagree with those representing the cause of other principles at the same time – hence two or more reputable participants may be present in the debate and may disagree at the prudential level, without there being any reason for either to regard the other as immoral, since each is respecting the constraints engendered by the fundamental purpose of a political politics. The situation is similar to that which obtains in an Anglo-Saxon court of law based upon the adversarial contest between prosecution and defence or litigant and plaintiff. The advocates on both sides are performing recognised and morally virtuous tasks necessary to the advance of the cause of justice; they can (and do) disagree without in the slightest accusing one another of evil practices; whereas, if either were to attack the standing of the court or the fundamental principles underlying its operation – for example, through the unbridled pursuit of the client's interest without regard for the rules of procedure – this would constitute an evil, since it would constitute an attack upon the conduct of justice itself. As in law courts, so in politics. Participants will typically disagree in their advocacy of different causes each of which deserve a hearing, and in their disagreement may both contribute to the morally valuable preservation of their shared civilisation; but the same participants may depart (through absolutism or unrestrained self-interest) from what is morally justified advocacy into acts which undermine the framework of the political life that protects civilisation, and hence may enter the field of the immoral. In short, the distinction between political politics (civilisation in the service of itself) and the practice of absolutist or barbaric crypto-politics becomes the distinguishing point between prudential difference and moral difference.

The remaining problem in this area with which the thesis has to deal is the Wilberforce phenomenon: why and how is it that we can so definitely identify Wilberforce's action in freeing the slaves as morally good rather than merely as prudentially advantageous? Here, too, the thesis provides a clear answer. The two vital features of slavery were: its disregard of one of the great principles within our civilisation (the principle of freedom) and the fact that this disregard was finally based not upon concern for some other principle such as beauty, truth or general prosperity, even if some of its advocates attempted so to argue, but rather upon naked self-interest. And these facts, enough in themselves to convict slavery of immorality, at the same time identify the contribution made by the abolition of slavery to the preservation of civilisation, and hence the moral quality of such abolition. A society with slavery is less civilised than one without slavery, because it is less free; the abolition of slavery makes a society, in this respect, more civilised; and the promotion of the civilisation is *ipso facto* (in contrast to the advocacy of particular, conflicting principles within a civilisation) morally right.

An interesting general point emerges here about the conduct of politics in a civilised society. It is at the same time, both very necessary and very difficult to distinguish between the proper advocacy of a principle and the advocacy of unrestrained self-interest – and very necessary but very difficult to distinguish between the advocacy of a principle and an absolutist attack upon the framework of society's civilisation. Typically, the evil proponents of unrestrained self-interest will disguise their propositions as advocacy of a principle (the equation of 'my prosperity' with 'prosperity', of 'beauty-for-me' with 'beauty', of 'freedom-for-me' with 'freedom'), and the distinction becomes increasingly difficult to make as the number of persons making the proposition enlarges as a proportion of the society as a whole. Typically, also, the absolutist will argue the cause of his favourite principle without mentioning that the measures he proposes will wholly or almost wholly disregard the claims of other principles. Lenin did not speak openly of the need to ignore the claims of truth in pursuit of the claims of equality. There are accordingly two opposing dangers both of which have to be resisted: the danger of assuming self-interest or absolutism in every opponent, hence widening too far the scope of the supposedly immoral; and the danger on the other side of taking at face value oratory that aims to disguise self-interest and absolutism, thus in fact ignoring the immoral when it is present.

The conduct of civilised, truly political politics depends upon an adequate resistance to both of these temptations.

The problem of other countries

As well as explaining the relationship between politics and ethics and the existence of so many ostensibly wrong theories about the ultimate aim of politics, the thesis that the ultimate aim of politics is the preservation of civilisation has a third advantage at the theoretical level: it can – as illustrated in Chapter 6 – provide a coherent account of the nature and limits of proper action in the sphere of international relations. By identifying the preservation of civilisation as the ultimate aim of all proper political action, the thesis explains: (1) the strong reasons, notwithstanding the absence of any straightforwardly identifiable legal basis, for the maintenance of mutual respect between one state and another, each enshrining its particular, civilised way of life which, for a lover of civilisation is *ipso facto* worthy of respect; (2) the occasional justification for intervention, where a foreign society has so broken down as to require the restoration of a framework of law which will rapidly and not too destructively restore the society to a state of peace within which civilised life can continue; (3) the more frequent justification for self-defence, where one's own society is under attack; and (4) the existence of strict limits upon the performance of any action on the international scene – limits which derive not from a system of international law but rather, directly from the necessity of behaving in certain ways (or more particularly of *not* behaving in certain ways) if the ultimate aim of preserving and promoting civilised life is not to be compromised by the manner of the act.

These are, of course, advantages only if one takes it as read that there *are* strong reasons for general respect between nations, occasional intervention, more frequent self-defence, and the constant observance (even in the event of intervention or self-defence) of certain constraints upon the nature of the actions taken. But such attitudes are, in fact, commonly accepted in Western liberal democracies: there is, in our societies, a strong pre-disposition in favour of peaceful co-existence; at the same time, there is widespread support for interventions such as those in Grenada or Bosnia; and there is an almost universal horror of entanglements in which either the brutality of the action itself or the incidental effects of it upon a society in which it takes place contravene the limits upon the nature of intervention. The missing element in the discussion of such episodes is not, therefore, typically the lack of a particular consensus on the appropriate attitude but, rather, an almost complete absence of a rational conceptual framework within which to carry on the discussion. Actions in the international field are typically defended or attacked either on the grounds of naked national self-interest or on the basis of fully fledged imperialism misdescribed as 'humanitarianism'. Neither of these theories answers to the true motives of the actors – the one being too narrow and cynical, the other too justificatory of perpetual intervention to coincide with the limited but definite acceptance of a degree of well-judged and limited interference in the affairs of other states. The introduction of the concept of transcendent politics – a realm of political action aimed at restoring civilisation and conditioned by its relation to that aim – has the merit not of making us think differently, but rather of explaining what we already think. To put the matter another way, the thesis that politics has as its ultimate aim the preservation of civilisation can make sense of attitudes which, though sincerely and widely held, can otherwise appear contradictory and chaotic.

Beyond providing such explanatory power, however, the thesis has a further advantage in the field of international relations. It serves not only to explain our attitudes to international interference and self-defence but also to explain the existence of variety. If the ultimate aim of politics were some abstract goal of the sort typically advanced by political theorists – whether justice, virtue, prosperity or any such – and if, as might indeed be the case, it could be shown that this abstract goal would be most likely to be fulfilled by the abolition of discrete states, the integration of all nationalities into a single state with one language, one set of universal laws and practices and so forth, then, on the usual theories, this would undoubtedly be a good thing. Such fashions have in fact been promoted from time to time by a wide range of proponents on the spectrum from the severely practical (as, for example, the invention of Esperanto) to the severely theoretical (of which Kant is the most distinguished exemplar). But, to almost all of us, there seems something obviously wrong with such integration: we *like* diversity, we *want* the richness of difference; we *lament* the increasing homogeneity of the world. And these attitudes – incomprehensible or at least indefensible if the true ultimate aim of politics happens to demand enlightened global union – are entirely understandable and defensible if, instead of consisting in such an abstract goal, the true ultimate aim of politics is the preservation of civilisation. For to love civilisation is to love it in its richness and its diversity, to love it in its many manifestations, and to lament any reduction in the number or variety of civilisations. He who aims at civilisation is thus an expansionist rather than a reductionist – needing always to be persuaded that the singularity of differing practices, differing civilised modes of life, can be preserved in any political homogenisation which may be desired for particular reasons (e.g. to promote particular principles) within the societies seeking such homogenisation. As in the case of international interference, the thesis of this book can, in other words, explain to us our already-held beliefs about the relationships of one society to the 'other'.

The provision of such explanations of attitudes already held, may seem a purely theoretical advantage: but, in the realm of politics, it is not so. 'Wrong' theories – in the sense of theories which do not answer to or explain the coherence of the pre-theoretical attitudes of civilised persons – may nevertheless come to dominate over those pre-theoretical attitudes and hence distort political action. Those who followed the Red Guard may very well on the whole have held, before coming under their sway, the highest respect for beauty and truth; their dogged pursuit of the destruction of great swathes of the beautiful and the true was nevertheless strongly influenced, if not indeed wholly brought about, by their conversion to a new way of seeing the matter – the re-description of works of art and science as heretical and idolatrous. Theories, in short, count. The Pope has armies. Accordingly, the recognition of the preservation of civilisation as the ultimate aim of politics serves the purpose not merely of explaining our attitudes to ourselves but also of giving us confidence in a coherent defence of those attitudes, and hence of protecting us from the appeal of facile and dangerous sloganising. The practical defence against bad theory in politics is not lack of theory, but good theory. The practical defence against the corruption of attitudes is the coherent defence of attitudes.

The challenge of the underclass

Both the inter-penetration of theory and practice in political action, and the particular advantages of the thesis that the preservation of civilisation is the ultimate aim of politics, are abundantly manifest in the vexed, the ghastly and the morally troubling problem of the underclass.

The existence in the societies of the modern 'developed' world of an underclass is a phenomenon more and more widely remarked in recent years. The defining characteristic of the underclass is not, of course, its poverty – the poor have, as the callous cliché has it, always been with us. The special and new phenomenon is the presence within our societies of a large number of persons who are fundamentally alienated from the civilisations of which those societies are the embodiments. Of course, alienation in one sense or another is no more a novelty than is poverty: one does not have to subscribe to the generalities of Marxist theory to accept that the medieval serf was in some important sense alienated from the products of his labour, or indeed that the worker in the Victorian poor-house may have been alienated by sentiment from the 'wealthy' and educated grandees who were its governors. Alienation from the civilisation of which one's own society is an expression, is, however, a radically different matter from other forms of social maladjustment or antipathy. The term 'one's own society' is important here: there is nothing new or special in the existence of refugees or migrants – individuals who, finding themselves in an alien land, find themselves also alien to its language, customs and practices, religion and the like; but to be an alien in *one's own* society, not to share in the civilisation, the language, the practices, values which constitute and emerge from that civilisation (and hence to be in a universal sense alienated, an alien everywhere and at home nowhere) *is* in its ghastliness both new and special.

Does such radical alienation truly exist in our societies? That it does is perhaps best illustrated by the contrast between a drugged adolescent in a modern inner city and a medieval serf. In terms of poverty, the modern adolescent is vastly the better-off of the two: instead of eking out a subsistence with the ever-present prospect of illness and death, the modern youth is supported in one way or another by the state in conditions which, whilst distasteful to the middle classes and quite possibly to himself, would nevertheless represent unimaginable luxury to the medieval serf. Nor is this merely a matter of absolute welfare: from a relative point of view, too, the modern youth will be vastly more nearly the *equal* of the rich than was the serf – who, by law, owned nothing, was himself in some sense a possession, and could not even freely direct the use of his own labour. But, despite these advantages compared to the serf, the drugged modern youth is – from the point of view of his relationship to his own civilisation – decisively more a stranger, an alien, than the serf. The serf, like his lord, gazed out on a landscape of untarnished beauty. Like his lord, he worshipped in a church that gathered him in its ritual and gave to him, however dimly, an intimation of the deepest longings and the most profound philosophy of his age and place. Like his lord, he acknowledged the legitimacy of the court at which elders would settle disputes on the basis of things known since 'time out of mind'. Like his lord, his life was fashioned by the great festivals of Christmas and Easter and harvest, and by the great events of baptism, marriage, burial. In short, the serf, despite his poverty and illiteracy and bondage, was reasonably at home in his own society, living a life fashioned by his own civilisation, a life within which the values of his civilisation were at the same time his values. The drugged, inner-city modern youth, by contrast, lives in a society in many ways more richly endowed, but shares almost none of that endowment; unlike his working-class or middle-class counterpart, he typically has no acquaintance with either the science or the art which in their immensity and magnificence constitute the great cultural achievements of his civilisation. At the same time, he lacks the natural rhythms and harmonies which fashioned the life of the illiterate serf – a share in rural beauty, customary law, religious observance. As a result, so far from sharing the values of his civilisation, he shares only the values of his gang or if, as sometimes, deprived even of that solicitude, no identifiable values at all. Of course, this description cannot be generalised: many relatively impoverished young people living in the inner cities of 'developed' western nations are very far from conforming to this bleak

picture; but the description nevertheless identifies a recognisable type – such alienation *does* exist.

The fact of such alienation is widely recognised as a phenomenon far more disturbing even than poverty. Indeed, it is
so troubling that it provokes in the remainder of the community either extreme anguish and hence urgent attempts to
cure it, or else a retreat into the 'nicer' parts of the country in
the hope that the inner city can be forgotten. For proponents
of the incomplete definitions of the aim of politics, identifying politics as aiming simply at, for example, justice, equality,
freedom, beauty, truth or prosperity, the dreadfulness of cultural alienation is difficult to explain. True, the alienated
'underclass' becomes a class to the extent that the alienated
members of it fail, in the course of their lives, to enter the
mainstream and instead become the progenitors of others
like themselves – the so-called 'cycle of deprivation'. True,
this represents for the proponents of every explanation of the
ultimate aim of politics, an aberration. The underclass represents an extreme case of inequality and an extreme failure to
contribute to the advance of beauty, truth and prosperity;
moreover, it can be argued that the existence of such a class
arises from, or at least constitutes a form of, injustice. But
from any of these points of view, there is nothing *uniquely*
ghastly about the alienation which the underclass represents.
Other members of society, not so alienated from the practices and values of their own civilisation, may be as poor and
hence as much an example of inequality; others may do as
little to contribute to the beauty or to appreciate the beauty
of their surroundings; others may perpetrate massive injustice
– and hence do more than the underclass to diminish the

propensity of the society towards truth, prosperity and justice. The utter ghastliness of the form of life which the members of the underclass are compelled to live – the sense in which their life is far worse than that of the medieval serf – can be explained only by a theory which acknowledges the fact that those who live it are alienated from their own civilisation. Once attention is focused on civilisation as the ultimate aim of politics, the peculiar unpleasantness of a life led as an alien from civilisation by one who should be a member of it becomes readily identifiable. The existence of an underclass represents a near-total failure of politics. If the preservation and enhancement of a civilisation is the aim of the politics of a society, then a society that permits the continued existence of an entire class alienated from that civilisation has – politically – failed. Nor can such failures be remedied merely by addressing the superficial accompaniments of the alienation – the poverty, the physical conditions of life. If the preservation of civilisation rather than of any single principle within it is the aim, then the challenge is to find a means of overcoming the alienation itself by bringing the underclass into connection with their own civilisation. The meeting of that challenge becomes – if the thesis of this book is correct – one of the great urgencies of our times, a task in the completion of which almost no effort can be too great, no ingenuity wasted, no sacrifice unjustified.

It may be argued that the logic here is in the wrong order – that, in other words, the critical nature of the challenge of the underclass is an implication of, rather than something that provides any evidential support for, the validity of the thesis that the preservation of civilisation is the ultimate aim of politics. But this argument, like its counterpart in connection with our attitudes to 'other' countries, misses the point. The advantage of the thesis is its ability to explain the attitude we take to the fate of the underclass. The thesis explains, in other words, the vast difference which we all see between the condition (however arduous) of the medieval serf and the condition of the drugged modern youth in the inner city. And, as with the problem of 'other' countries, the thesis – by explaining the attitudes we already share, also brings more clearly to light the appropriate form of response, indicates more clearly the depth of the problem that we all feel needs to be resolved and the futility of merely treating its superficial accompaniments.

The conflict of freedom and community
The challenge of the underclass, for all its desperate practical importance, is in truth no more than the most striking and poignant example of a problem which is in fact deeper and more universal: the conflict between freedom and community. This is, if anything is, *the* problem of our times. It is in providing at least a way of thinking about this problem that the thesis of this book – the thesis that politics, properly conceived, is civilisation in the service of itself – finally comes into its own and finds its justification.

The gospel of the West is the gospel of freedom, and the miracle of the West is the life of the free. The images of Prometheus, the David and the Statue of Liberty are to us the central images of humanity. Even if we do not agree with it, we can make sense of the existentialist proposition that humanity expresses its identity, marks itself off from the animal kingdom, in the very act of free choice without regard for the outcome or conditions of such choice: indeed, the identification of human activity with the expression of Will is in a number of variants a recurrent (even if persistently heterodox) view of Western philosophy. This fundamental attachment to freedom is no accident. It arises not merely from the fact that freedom is one of the principles of our civilisation, but also from the instrumental role that freedom plays in relation to other principles. The unfettered spirit is expressed in, and is a precondition for, the great works of art and science – the great contributions to beauty and truth – which constitute so notable a facet of our civilisation. The theory of Forms is the brainchild – and hence also the will-child – of its Plato; the Sistine Chapel of its Michelangelo; the theory of relativity of its Einstein. These crowning achievements arise when man, in the uniqueness of his liberty to think and feel, draws from the depths of his individuality a new, a particular way of thinking, seeing, understanding.

To say this about freedom is, however, to say at once too much and not enough. For such statements carry with them – if left unadorned – the implication, wholly false, that the unchannelled spirit of the atomic individual represents the fullest fulfilment of human potential. The reality is, of course, wholly contrary. Atomic individuality is at one level a self-contradiction and at another a description of Hell: a contradiction because individuality (of a more than merely physical variety) emerges from the ability of the individual to create himself as a character – an ability made possible only through fully fledged cognition that itself depends upon symbolic language and hence depends also upon society; and a description of Hell, because we humans can be content only in the giving and receiving of affection – a giving and receiving that is possible only in and through society. These are facts understood not only in the East, with its ready acceptance of the primacy of society, but also in the West. Our religions and our philosophies, even those that emphasise most poignantly the heroic individual and the yearning for freedom, have always, except in the parodies of their detractors, taken into account the forces of our affections for others and the social origin of our cognition.

We come here face to face with the fundamental paradox of the human predicament: the contradictory interdependence, within civilisation, of freedom and community. Freedom – one of the absolute principles of our civilisation – has its meaning only within a community of language, of value, of affection; but that same freedom includes the freedom to leave, to disengage, worse yet to disrupt or destroy the community in which its subject subsists. This paradox is obvious, and has been remarked by every serious commentator of every variety, philosophical, theological, psychological, anthropological and sociological since time immemorial. It is played out daily in our ordinary existence in the contrast of our longings to be independent, and at the same time to belong, and even more powerfully in the contrast between our anger at constriction and our dread of loneliness. These conflicting emotions – the longing to be free versus the longing to belong, anger at constraint versus the dread of loneliness – are the polarities of our affections; we live our lives strung between them, pulled the one way and the other

– towards and away from marriage, family, friends, firms, colleges, clubs and monasteries. Accordingly, much political theory has been devoted either to denying the 'real' existence of a conflict between freedom and community (crudely, the purpose of at least the Lockean theory of Natural Law); or to asserting the supremacy of one over the other (crudely, the purpose of Hobbes from one direction and of the libertarians from the other); or to envisaging a social order within which the conflict can be transformed into a willing conformity of individual within community (crudely, the project in differing ways of the different strands of Hegelian and post-Hegelian theory). But each of these theoretical projects remains just that – a brave but vain attempt to theorise away a tension which stubbornly persists in our politics, as much in the lives of our affections.

The advantage of the thesis that the ultimate aim of politics is to preserve civilisation is that it accommodates, one might almost say protects, the existence of the paradox and thereby removes the need to theorise away the problem. If freedom has its place as one of the principles of our civilisation, and if civilisation is *ipso facto* a social, communal phenomenon, then it is to be expected that the tension between freedom and the community which at the same time creates and constrains freedom will be permanent and irremediable. The tension has the same pattern as that which – if the thesis of this book is correct – obtains in the case of tensions between other principles such as equality and prosperity, virtue and justice, beauty and truth; but the tension between freedom and community is the most fundamental of all because freedom (like the other principles, at the same time

a product of and a contribution to the civilisation) is also –
unlike the others, continuously a disruptive force, threatening the dissolution of the social. It is a Trojan horse built by
the Trojans, an expression of civilisation which is at the same
time the vehicle for barbarism. In short, the tension, in this
one case, is a tension not merely between two facets of civilisation but between civilisation and itself. Politics, if it is to be
conceived as civilisation in the service of itself, must have as
its prime transient aim the continuous establishment of contingent resolution of *this* tension, the continuous achievement of temporary, practical resolutions between the
demands of community and the demands of freedom, the
demands of civilisation-Jekyll and of civilisation-Hyde.

It is here, at last, that the deep truth lying behind the
confused meandering which has been called 'communitari-
anism' is to be found. For community itself, the fact-of-
living-together-harmoniously, is not merely a precondition
for the existence of civilisation, but also – in its affective
aspect – a principle in its own right. We *want* to live in a society within which politics continuously finds contingent resolutions not only between the conflicting claims of each
abstract desideratum to which each civilisation gives absolute
value but also between any such absolutes (above all, in this
context, freedom) and the desire – in itself an absolute – to
make possible the fact-of-living-together-harmoniously. In
other words, the communitarian can be recognised as no
more and no less than the advocate of a particular principle:
not a theoretician endowed with a philosophy, but a legitimate participant in political debate pointing to the importance of something long-recognised which may nevertheless

have been overly neglected in the practical political discussions of Western civilisation in recent years.

8 What Next?

Recognitions and obligations

A long and wise tradition of philosophers from Aristotle to Oakeshott has taught us that having the practical skill of knowing how to cook is not the same thing as being able to read the recipes of cookery books. The conduct of politics being somewhat more complex than cookery, it is not to be expected that any thesis formulated in political theory will provide a precise recipe for immediate application. Accordingly, the thesis of this book does not prescribe particular political acts – still less, the adoption of a particular political policy or the support of a particular political party in a particular country at a particular time. The thesis cannot pretend, however, to the Olympian detachment of a true philosophical, mathematical, historical, or scientific proposition: unlike such reflections, rather than pure analysis, it offers recommendations – it contains an 'ought'. Indeed, it contains an 'ought' that is unconditional, and hence moral in nature, demanding obedience, regardless of motive: an 'ought' the observance of which, alone, can in the long run preserve what is most valuable in the world.

The 'ought' implied by the proposition is composed, of course, in its unconditionality of adverbial rather than substantive prescriptions. It dictates a 'how', not a 'what'. And the 'how' in this case is concerned with politics not with private conduct – it prescribes how those who act in politics (the statesman or official administering, the politician politicking, the journalist writing or interviewing, the activist lobbying, the citizen voting) should act when engaged in politics rather than how the same persons should act in their private lives. Hence, whilst moral in its unconditionality, it is strictly confined to the realm of public activity: it can be observed by persons who are, in a wider sense, bad; but no-one who fails to observe it, when entering the public arena, can claim to be entirely good.

The 'ought' prescribes, in the first place, the recognitions required in all political argument: (1) the recognition of the transience and potential equivalence of all political positions; (2) the consequent recognition of accepted procedure as superior to the achievement of transient aims, because of the fact that such procedure is a precondition for the achievement of the peaceful resolutions between principles without which civilised life cannot continue; and also, (3) the recognition of the legitimacy of advocacy by others of other principles and hence of other and perhaps conflicting transient aims.

Next, the 'ought' prescribes the duty to distinguish: (1) the duty to distinguish the civilised and constructive advocates of opposing principles from the absolutists, the visionary scientists, the rationalists, the millenarians, the barbarians and the crowd all too easily swayed by any or all of these destructive crypto-political characters; (2) even more difficult, the duty to distinguish times when politics as a constructive art can continue to be pursued owing to the sufficient presence of others willing to engage in the civilised pursuit of conditional accommodations and temporary resolutions, from the moment when such politics becomes impossible and only transcendent politics can remedy the situation – the moment, in short, when the ploughshare must give way to the sword.

Arising out of these general prescriptions to recognise and to distinguish, the 'ought' contains more precisely and concretely a number of proscriptions: it proscribes every act or form of act that belies the recognitions and distinctions – hence all acts and forms of act which militate against the conduct of the civilised debate that alone permits the achievement of contingent resolutions between principles. Under this heading, it proscribes many practices which have become usual and even expected: the demeaning of politics by the triviality, cynicism and shallowness that characterises, on occasion, the utterances of politicians themselves, and all too frequently characterises the activities of journalism in its widest sense – the turning of politics into a bullfight.

Finally, and most importantly, the 'ought' contains a recommendation which, whilst still adverbial rather than directly substantive, nevertheless touches clearly on the substantive – a recommendation about the image of society that all those engaged in public life should carry in their heads. It is in the first place an image in which each society is itself understood as an artefact of inestimable worth, a fabric kaleidoscopically related to those larger civilisations within which it subsists and those civilised societies contiguous with it in time and space. It is an image in which the modulated observance of accepted procedures appears not as a luxury but as the sole means of achieving, without destruction of the fabric, continuously emerging contingent resolutions between principles which are each absolute and between which there are continuously emerging conflicts in practice. Persons who carry in their heads this image will be constant, in the sense that their political actions will be governed by the constant pursuit of an intelligible end; but they will not be univocal – as new voices are heard, as new concerns capture the imagination and pull the fabric in one direction or another, they will recall the absolutes that stand in danger of being forgotten, the principles whose force is temporarily not being felt or not being sufficiently felt, and they will become proponents of those principles.

What today, in our Western civilisation, are the principles in danger of being forgotten, the principles that need proponents?

The political problem of virtue

In the first place, and most evidently, there is a lack of virtue. To say this is not, of course to be dewy-eyed about the state of affairs in previous ages or other places. There has, no doubt, been always and everywhere (except in the pre-lapsarian Garden of Eden) a lack of virtue in the sense of a falling away from perfection: whether sin is or is not original, it is certainly pervasive. But there is nevertheless evidence that a great part of Western civilisation is threatened – that is to say, in a great many places in the West, the conduct of a civilised life is threatened – by a lack of virtue more exaggerated than at some other times and in some other places. The evidence in question is the prevalence of crime.

One enters, here, a morass of conflicting definition and analysis: 'what is crime?', 'to what extent has it, or has some variant of it (if, in any case, comparable across times and places) really been greater at some times and places than others?', 'to what extent is the presence or absence of crime a measure of the presence or absence of virtue and to what extent is it a measure instead of the presence or absence of fear of retribution?', and so forth. But there stands, above this morass, a great signpost that points unmistakably in a particular direction. In most of New York in 1800, or most of London in 1950, one could confidently have hung out in a string bag for collection by a delivery boy a payment for household deliveries; in 1997 – even if delivery boys were still in plentiful supply – it would have been folly to attempt such an endeavour in either London or New York. For this change, there may be many explanations – but one amongst them is certainly that the expectation of virtue (that is to say, the expectation that almost all persons almost all of the time will be governed by self-disciplined adhesion to certain not necessarily very elevated but nevertheless important rules of behaviour) used at those times in those places to be high, and is now low. And it would take a heroic degree of argumentative disposition to make someone want to claim that the change in expectation is due entirely to an increased scepticism about the behaviour of other persons rather than, in the slightest degree, to a change in that behaviour itself. The plain truth is that certain forms of virtue, which used in certain places at certain times to be taken for granted because they were in fact widespread, are now in those same places assumed to be absent because they are in fact frequently absent.

To anyone who knows the meaning of the term 'virtue',

and who is not determined to be perverse, the proposition that this lack of virtue needs remedying requires no defending. It is, in the proper sense, self-evident that – *ceteris paribus* – an increase in virtue is to be desired and a diminution of virtue is to be avoided. There is, moreover, no need to concern ourselves, here, with questions of moral relativism since the virtue in question that is missing is regarded as virtue within the society where it is missing and was also so regarded when it was more widely prevalent. Some of a commodity which is understood within the context of 'our' civilisation as desirable in itself is less prevalent than it was – and this is, to put it at its most banal, a Bad Thing.

But, beyond the absolute undesirability of the diminution of certain forms of virtue, it is instrumentally undesirable that this diminution should have occurred: an absence of virtue has, in other words, undesirable consequences as well as being undesirable in itself. One need not pause, here, to consider whether this also painfully banal observation is, to a degree at least, definitional (i.e. whether there is an intrinsic connection between the classification of certain types of action as virtuous and the instrumental advantages for society of those types of action). The important point for our present purposes is rather that – regardless of whether this is a tautology or an empirical observation – virtue on the part of the citizen has an instrumental value for his fellow citizens. To put the point at its simplest, a society in which what we in 'our' civilisation regard as virtuous action is widespread will be a society within which it is easier to live a civilised life – will, *ceteris paribus*, be a more civilised society – than one in which the citizens pass their days in fear of attack, or of depredation by evil-doers. To put the point at its most extreme, the Hobbesian war of each against all (the ultimate antithesis of civilisation) is more likely to prevail where what we regard as virtue is wholly absent, and a state of peace (the friend of civilised discourse, of civilised conduct and of the advancement of civilisation) is more likely to prevail where what we regard as virtue is present. If we begin with acceptance of these three propositions – that virtue is notably in short supply in our societies at present, that virtue is self-evidently of absolute value within the civilisation where it is recognised as virtue, and that what we in 'our' (in a very broad sense of 'our') civilisation regard as virtue is also of instrumental value to the preservation of that civilisation – then it follows from the thesis that the ultimate aim of politics is to preserve civilisation that it should be a major aim of modern politics within 'our' societies to increase the virtuousness of the citizenry. But we encounter a problem, or rather a maze of problems. In the first place, there is as ever the problem of conflicting principles – in this case, the conflict between virtue and freedom arising from the fact that any attempt to inculcate virtue in an individual almost inevitably depends on inculcating habits through curtailing over a long initiation the range of action, in particular the range of evil action, of that individual. It should be stressed that there is in the *outcome* no tension between freedom and virtue, since the virtuous person remains free to act as he chooses. But the restraint involved in the formation of habits that permit virtue to exist, and hence the tension between the inculcation of such habits and freedom, is undeniable. A society that seeks to inculcate virtue in its citizens cannot avoid imposing some of the constraints of the schoolroom.

This, then, is the practical problem of virtue in our time: we face in two directions, pulled towards the schoolroom of virtue by the desire to promote virtuous dispositions and pulled away from it by the allure of the open fields of freedom. What is more, to add to the conflict of principles we find ourselves in a practical quandary created by what has been called the 'moral ignorance' of the state. Even if a lack of virtue in many Western societies is recognised by the citizenry as a whole, and even if this recognition is shared by those responsible for the governance of the state, it does not follow that those governors have – either singly or collectively – the capacity to determine with accuracy the steps that would need to be taken to remedy that lack of virtue. Schooling in any art or science is a matter of the greatest subtlety, and the record of the state in facilitating the provision of more, or rather of more effective, education in the arts and sciences than would have occurred without its intervention is, at best, patchy. But schooling in virtue is an altogether more difficult and subtler task – one which taxes to the extreme the spiritual and practical resources of great schools and wise parents. Reforming those schools that are not great or even good and those parents who are not wise, in the face of apparent indifference or opposition, in order to affect the moral training of their children in a fashion which sensibly increases their chances of attaining virtue, are challenges of such practical difficulty as to raise questions about the possibility and wisdom of the undertaking – even if one imagines away for an instant the likelihood of conflict with the requirements of freedom. We lack, in short, the confidence of

Plato in the availability of Guardians of sufficient wisdom.

The political problem of beauty

The political problem of virtue is, however, no more acute or irresolvable than the political problem of beauty: and the description of ugliness as sinful – whilst strictly a category mistake – illustrates vividly not only the ghastliness of ugliness but also the similarity in impoverishment of a world deprived of virtue and a world deprived of beauty. One of the great sustaining circumstances of human existence is the existence of the beautiful; its absence renders life but a dank and drab affair. In both cases – a society deprived of virtue and a society deprived of beauty – the deficiency cries out for a remedy. And, as with virtue, the *fact* of a deficiency is uncontroversial: our eyes are assaulted by the excrescences of barren, filthy cityscapes and despoiled countryside; and this is not merely a static catastrophe – the sustained destruction over the past century in many parts of the world of the beautiful, both natural and man-made, offers the grim prospect, if it continues, of a world immeasurably aesthetically impoverished. But, as with virtue, the search for a remedy is impeded by the tension between principles and by a practical difficulty. The tension is, as in the case of virtue, between the preservation of the beautiful and the constraints that this imposes upon the freedom of the uglifier. And, even if this tension is temporarily ignored on the grounds that beauty's voice in the argument has not been sufficiently heard and should be given a greater say, there remains a practical problem strictly analogous to the moral ignorance which hampers governors in any attempt to school the citizen in virtue

– namely, the aesthetic ignorance of the state, perhaps even more dismal in its completeness than the state's moral ignorance.

These two difficulties are, indeed, particularly acute in the modern state because – although there may be a considerable measure of agreement about the ugly some time after it has been created – there is all too often little agreement in advance of, or contemporaneously with, the event. This heightens both the tensions with freedom and the practical likelihood that the state, in its aesthetic ignorance, will produce damaging rather than advantageous results. Frequent debates about the right or lack of right of firms or individuals to erect arguably beautiful skyscrapers are an example of the tension; and the widespread establishment throughout the major cities of the world of what are now generally regarded as appallingly ugly municipal housing developments, many of which were, at the time of their construction, regarded as at least by some as models of progress and beauty, is a vivid testimony to the effects of the aesthetic ignorance of the state. We face, in other words, an apparently intractable problem almost daily in its occurrence: a problem typically expressed in the especial disdain shown both towards the unbridled mania for development displayed by certain capitalists and towards the intervention of 'cultural commissars' of various types employed by the state.

Towards a solution?

There are some grounds for optimism that at least partial solutions to these two, at first glance intractable, problems may gradually be found. The critical advance consists of emphasising two distinctions – first, the distinction between the public and the private faces of human action; and second, the distinction between that which is inherited and that which is invented.

The relevance of the distinction between the public and private faces of action is perhaps most evident in relation to the beautiful and the ugly. The balance between the principle of freedom and the principle of beauty alters progressively as one moves along the continuum from the blatantly public (the building of a new road, the coating of the Reichstag in plastic) towards the hermetically private (the decoration of the inside lid of a music-box). This is not because the principle of beauty becomes weaker as one moves towards the private – indeed, for those who hear the call of the beautiful, it is as loud in private as in public affairs. Rather, the change of balance that occurs as one moves towards the private is a progressive increase in the force of the principle of freedom. To the extent that the affair is public, the freedom of the perpetrator must be set against other principles, of justice, equality and so forth, and the claim of freedom is accordingly diminished. To put this in another way, more immediately relevant to the political problem of beauty, as one moves towards the realm of the public, the public desire for the production of beauty comes to have a larger, and the principle of freedom a correspondingly smaller, claim. Or again, to put the matter in its negative form, as one moves from the public to the private, the claim of freedom, including the freedom to construct the ugly, becomes stronger because there is less support from other principles for the claim of beauty. Accordingly, one tentative move towards the resolution of the political problem of beauty is to emphasise politically the claim of beauty in relation to public rather than in relation to private life.

The same general principle, for the same general reasons – perhaps even more directly – can be applied in relation to the political problem of virtue. Considered as an absolute in its own right, the claim of virtue in private action is, of course, as great as in public action. But, as one moves from the hermetically private to the blatantly public, the claim of virtue is, as with the claim of beauty, much reinforced by its coincidence with the claims of other principles – most notably the principle of justice which, at any rate in some contexts, becomes the public face of virtue itself. Correspondingly, the principle of freedom – including freedom to be sinful – is at its strongest in the most private domain where the claim of virtue stands alone unsupported by explicitly public requirements for justice. Accordingly, as with the political problem of beauty, the beginning of a resolution of the political problem of virtue may perhaps be found in a decision to emphasise the 'public' or civic aspects of virtue – a decision in other words to emphasise politically the applications of virtuous motives in situations where the consequences are public or nearly public acts, leaving the inculcation of virtue in the private sphere more nearly to private institutions.

The second distinction, between that which is inherited and that which is invented, helps to resolve another aspect of the political problems of freedom and beauty – not so much the *sphere* within which politics can act vis-à-vis virtue and beauty without overtly ignoring the claim of freedom, but rather the *basis* upon which politics, when it is enforced in the public sphere, can found its assertion of the beautiful and virtuous as opposed to the ugly and vicious. In short, the distinction between inheritance and invention helps to resolve the practical problem posed by the aesthetic and moral ignorance of the state.

The essential proposition here is that what is inherited is *prima facie* worthy of preservation and that what is a more ancient inheritance is *prima facie* the more earnestly to be preserved, and that the state without pretending to any particular moral or aesthetic knowledge can more safely intervene to protect that which is an ancient inheritance than to protect that which is newly invented. The grounds for this proposition are multifold. In the first place, there is a fundamental argument that inherited practice is the foundation of civilisation and that a politics whose proper aim is the preservation of civilisation must pay at all times especial heed to the preservation of such inheritances. Second, there is the argument from probability – that practices and items which have been preserved by generations before us are more likely to be virtuous or beautiful than not, since these same generations have had multiple opportunities to review the moral and aesthetic value of what they have bequeathed us and have collectively made the decision to preserve that which has been preserved. Third, there is the argument of the 'worst case' – that by preserving those things which are inherited, there is at least no loss, whereas by permitting their destruction by the novel, there may be irreparable harm. No one of these arguments is by itself conclusive: nor does the collection of the three arguments demonstrate in any irrefutable way the general validity of state intervention to preserve the inherited or the general invalidity of state intervention in favour of the novel in matters of beauty or virtue – any more than, for example, in the case of justice, where a simple refusal to do more than to enshrine the inherited could all too easily have been (and by some was) interpreted to argue against Wilberforce's use of the state to abolish slavery But there remains a degree of power in the three arguments – a power sufficient to suggest at least that the state is on firmer ground when its interventions in support of virtue and beauty not only relate to the public rather than the private faces of these attributes but also to the preservation of inherited practices and items rather than to the promotion of the newly invented.

The ceaseless round

These are then pointers towards the resolution of the political problems of virtue and beauty. But they are no more than pointers – and the resolutions are far off. At every opportunity, the voices clamouring for freedom and prosperity, in some cases also the voices of justice and equality, will be raised against the claims of virtue and beauty and against efforts by the state to intervene on behalf of virtue and beauty. Where is the resting point? When can we expect the argument to be finally won, by the one side or the other? When will these tensions be finally resolved? The answer is a string of negatives: none, never, never. There is no resting point, no end to the debate, no permanent resolution of the tensions. There is at best – because of the very nature of our civilisation – a fabric of contingent resolutions achieved through political discussion, each capable of further revision as the fabric is pulled this way and that by the conflicting demands inherent to our civilisation.

The preservation of civilisation by politics – the sacred task of politics – implies not rest, but perpetual movement. It is only in the harmonic antiphony of that ceaseless round that we can discover and rediscover our secular salvation.

Papers in Print

SMF Papers

Reports

Occasional Papers

Other Papers

Memoranda

Trident Trust/ SMF Contributions to Policy

3. *How Effective is Work Experience?*
   Greg Clark and Katharine
   Raymond (Foreword by Colin
   Cooke-Priest)
   £8.00

Hard Data

1. *The Rowntree Inquiry and 'Trickle
   Down'*
   Andrew Cooper, Roderick Nye
   £5.00

2. *Costing the Public Policy Agenda: A
   week of the* Today *Programme*
   Andrew Cooper
   £5.00

3. *Universal Nursery Education and
   Playgroups*
   Andrew Cooper, Roderick Nye
   £5.00

4. *Social Security Costs of the Social
   Chapter*
   Andrew Cooper, Marc Shaw
   £5.00

5. *What Price a Life?*
   Andrew Cooper, Roderick Nye
   £5.00

Centre for Post-Collectivist Studies

1. *Russia's Stormy Path to Reform*
   Robert Skidelsky (ed.)
   £20.00

2. *Macroeconomic Stabilisation in Russia:
   Lessons of Reforms, 1992–1995*
   Robert Skidelsky, Liam Halligan
   £10.00

3. *The End of Order*
   Francis Fukuyama
   £9.50

4. *From Socialism to Capitalism: What is
   meant by the 'Change of System'?*
   János Kornai
   £8.00

5. *The Politics of Economic Reform*
   Robert Skidelsky (ed.)
   £12.00

6. *The Rise and Fall of the Swedish
   Model*
   Mauricio Rojas
   £10.00

Briefings

1. *A Guide to Russia's Parliamentary
    Elections*
    Liam Halligan, Boris Mozdoukhov
    £10.00

SMF/Profile Books

1. *Is Conservatism Dead?*
    John Gray and David Willetts
    £8.99

2. *A Better State of Health*
    John Willman
    £8.99

3. *Will Europe Work?*
    David Smith
    £8.99